DANTE

The Invention of Celebrity

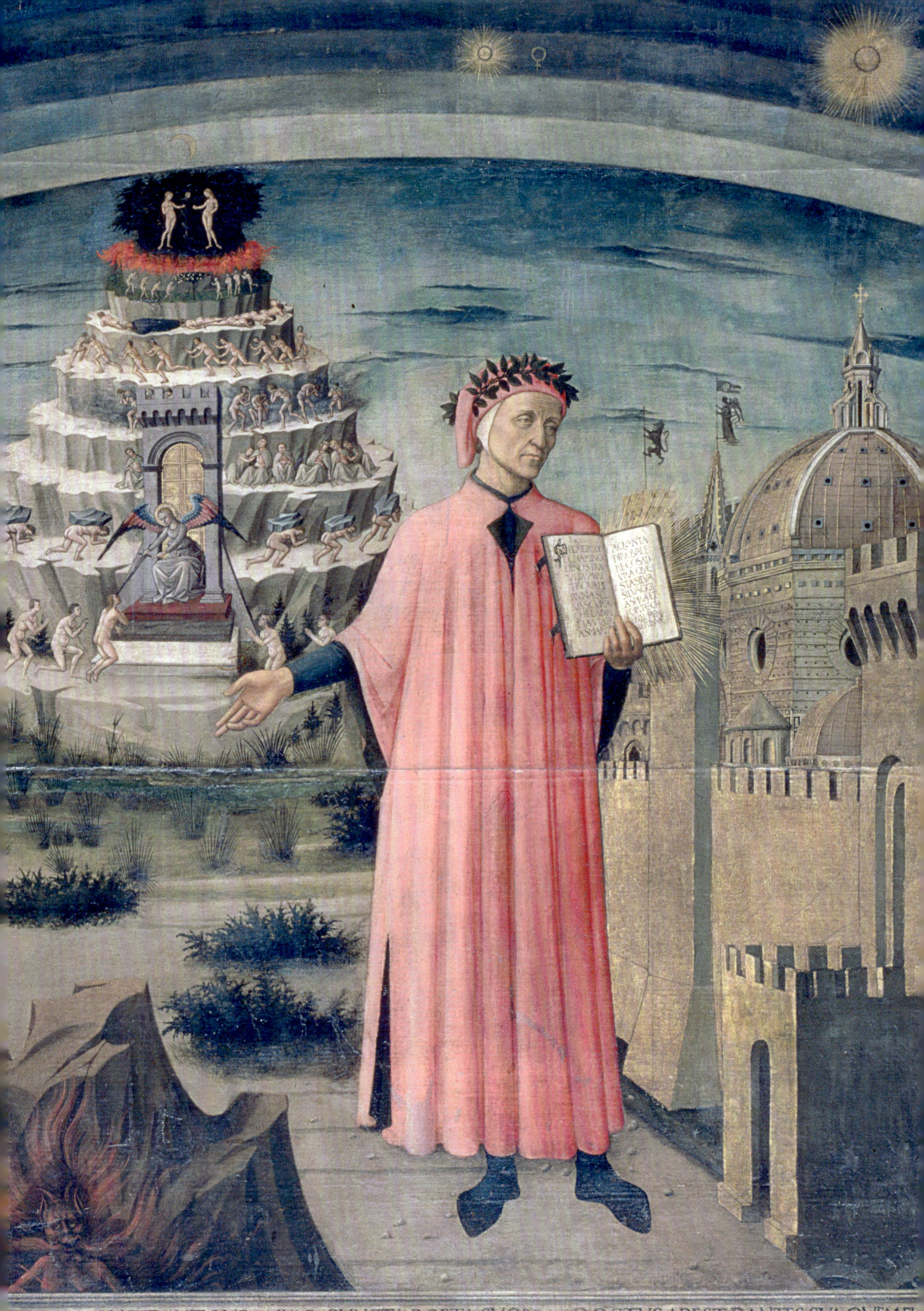
LVSTRAVITQVE ANIMO CVNCTA POETA SVO
DOCTVS ADEST DANTES SVA QVEM

DANTE

The Invention of Celebrity

Gervase Rosser

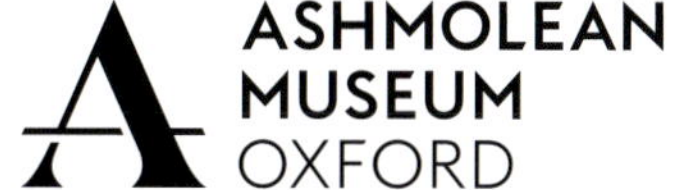

DANTE: THE INVENTION OF CELEBRITY

Copyright © Ashmolean Museum, University of Oxford, 2021

Gervase Rosser has asserted his moral right to be identified as the author of this work.

British Library Cataloguing in Publications Data

A catalogue record for this book is available from the British Library.

ISBN: 978-1-910807-49-1

All rights reserved. No part of this publication may be transmitted in any form or by any means, electronic or mechanical, including photocopy, recording or any storage and retrieval system, without the prior permission in writing of the publisher.

Designed by Stephen Hebron

Printed and bound in Great Britain by Gomer Press

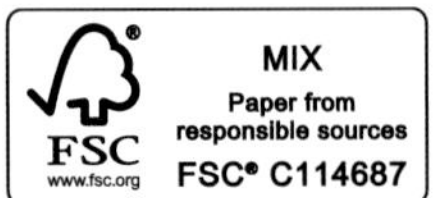

Cover: Ingrid Bergman observing a bust of Dante under a portico in Venice, 1955. Photograph by Mario Carrieri via Getty Images.

Frontispiece: Domenico di Michelino, *Dante and his poem the 'Divine Comedy'* (detail), 1465, tempera on panel, Florence Cathedral (© Raffaello Bencini / Bridgeman Images).

For further details of Ashmolean titles please visit: www.ashmolean.org/shop

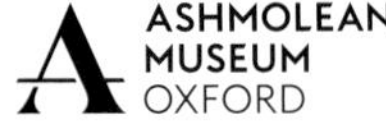

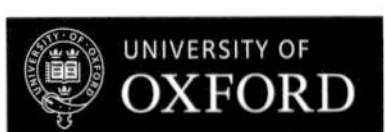

CONTENTS

'The central man of all the world' 7

Damned Celebrity; Fame Redeemed 8

The Image of the Poet 16

The Mirror of Fame: In Dante's Company 29

The Price of Fame: Commercial Dante 37

The Path to Fame in Popular Culture 40

Selected Highlights 51

Image: Work in Progress 56

Further Reading 64

Acknowledgements 64

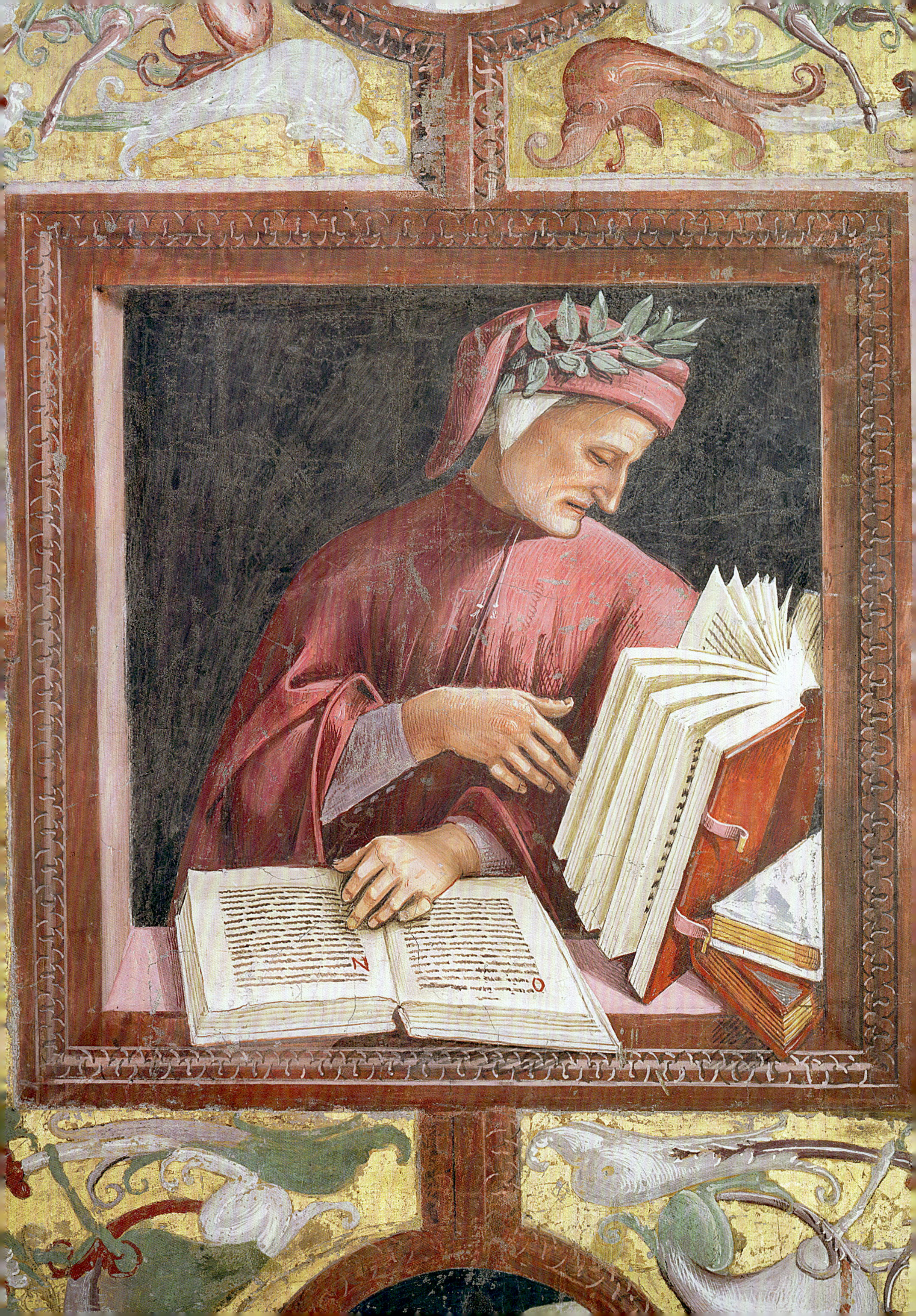

'THE CENTRAL MAN OF ALL THE WORLD'

John Ruskin's assessment of Dante Alighieri, printed in the early 1850s, has been echoed many times in the context not only of western but of global culture.[1] Our modern perception of greatness, less tied to a particular civilisational perspective, appreciates a multifaceted Dante, seen to be capable of speaking to diverse cultures in multiple dialects. Famous as the author of a poem, the *Comedy*, which describes his vision of Hell, Purgatory and Paradise, Dante also remains one of the most searching critics of fame itself.

Ours is an age of personality cults, of fashionistas, of instant and often unremarkable celebrities. Modern media have accelerated the construction of personal fame, which to a limited extent has also been democratised, as Andy Warhol prophesied: 'In the future, everyone will be world-famous for fifteen minutes'. Early predictions of the demise of celebrity culture as a consequence of the interruption of live performances during the Covid pandemic have proved to be premature, while *The X-Factor*, successors to *Big Brother*, the persona of the Internet blogger, and the Instagrammed selfie remain available to the less rich and famous as means to reach out for recognition from our fellow human beings.

Yet our desires are not so original – it is only our arrogance that leads us to think them to be so – and these staples of our modern world have an origin which lies deep in the European cultural past. In fact, it was Dante's *Comedy*, composed at the start of the fourteenth century, which, for the first time ever, dramatised the lives of ordinary people on a cosmic stage, with full revelation of their characters. At the core of the *Comedy* is the emblematic significance of the lives of individual persons, whatever their status. And by writing a poetic bestseller, Dante in turn became, himself, a celebrity. Given that outcome, it is easy to overlook the improbability of the phenomenon that was – and is – Dante. In the Italian peninsula around 1300 dozens wrote verse and thousands experienced political exile, yet only one used the first to translate the second into a poem which gained an instant reputation and continues to resonate around the world today. As the man who had been to Hell and back, who told truth to tyrants and exposed the corruption of popes, and whose own love story with Beatrice was the ultimate romance epic, Dante himself acquired the status of an icon. For – again – the very first time, an individual of no particular status became an international poster-boy for justice, liberty, and love. A sixteenth-century publisher would add the word *Divine* to the title of his poem, sealing the author's reputation beyond the ordinary run of mortals.

As a historical figure of fourteenth-century Italy, Dante has been canonised in a western cultural tradition; yet the *Comedy* has long broken those bounds, and its author today belongs to the world at large. Each new

Fig. 1 Luca Signorelli (1441–1523), *Dante*. San Brizio Chapel, Orvieto Cathedral, 1499–1504. By permission of the Opera of the cathedral of Orvieto. Photo © Raffaello Bencini / Bridgeman Images.

appropriation has been transformative. The first Japanese translation was made in 1914–16, shortly to be followed by the foundation of the Japanese Dante Society. A recent manga version, intended by its artist Go Nagai to reach a mass audience, incorporates elements from regional culture including Buddhism and Japanese cinema (see fig. 38). The influential Indian philosopher and poet Sri Aurobindo (1872–1950) in his epic *Savitri* rewrote stories from ancient Indian tradition from the perspective of Dante's *Comedy*. In *The System of Dante's Hell* (1965), the African-American writer LeRoi Jones (subsequently known as Amiri Baraka, 1934–2014) used a Dantesque allegory to describe a young black man's experience of segregation and prejudice in the southern United States. Twenty years later another African-American novelist, Gloria Naylor (1950–2016), would use Dante's *Inferno* as the structure of a fierce satire on the American dream. *Linden Hills* (1985) is set in an African American suburb, passage through which reveals progressively increasing material prosperity, larger houses, and deepening corruption as the occupants fall victim to the hollow ideals of American capitalism. The Nobel prize-winning poet Derek Walcott (1930–2017), whose birth in St Lucia gave him a critical perspective on European colonialism, found in Dante and Homer his two most significant literary influences. From the *Odyssey* and from Dante, Walcott drew inspiration for his own exploration of the theme of exile. The Argentinian Jorge Luis Borges (1899–1986), whose writings changed the course of Latin American and world literature, returned repeatedly to the author of the *Comedy*, the universality of which he underlined: 'Had I to name a single work as being at the top of all literature, I think I should choose the *Divina Commedia* by Dante. And yet I am not a Catholic'.[2]

DAMNED CELEBRITY; FAME REDEEMED

The modern world is familiar with an idea of fame which has roots in the stories and images of classical Greece and Rome. It has been a persistent characteristic of empire to put heroes on pedestals, and that usage has given rise, in our own postcolonial period, to a new critique of memorialising statues. The construction of personal fame has, however, a wider significance, which Dante was the first to subject to rigorous analysis.

Far older yet than Dante, of course, was Fame: that fickle, god-like power which makes or destroys reputation. Classical poetry and public statues constructed the glory of male heroes of the battlefield (Hector) or the intellect (Plato). At the same time, the ancients were aware of the corrosive effects of human forgetfulness or, worse, rumour, which could mar the standing of the most glorious. Dido and Aeneas, in Book IV of Virgil's *Aeneid*, suffer the slander of Rumour, described as a horrible 'monster' which spreads salacious stories in a 'mixture of fact and fiction'. Virgil's younger contemporary Ovid, in Book XII of his *Metamorphoses*, imagined the House of Rumour to be located in the centre of the world, where all tales could be heard, elaborated and redistributed with destructive consequences. In the house, 'rumours mingle in their thousands, the false with the true'. There has always been 'fake news', and the fragility of worldly reputation is something which has been taken for granted from ancient times.

Medieval Christianity complicated but did not altogether banish fame. Saint Augustine patronised pagans who hoped for the hollow reward of earthly fame, whereas Christians enjoyed the prospect of eternal glory in Heaven. Yet Dante, who like Augustine had read the Roman poets, developed a more complex relationship with worldly reputation. One potent classical idea to which Dante remained closely wedded was that of the poet as a prophet and guarantor of fame. Virgil achieved this for Aeneas, the hero of his *Aeneid*, which tells the story of the foundation of Rome, and by doing so the writer ensured his own eternal glory. That reputation explains Dante's affinity with Virgil and his choice of him as the character who, in the *Comedy*, would be his guide through the realms of Hell and Purgatory. When, in *Inferno*, Virgil relates to Dante how he had been recruited to this role, he reports that he was visited by Beatrice, who addressed him with words which acknowledged his renown on earth: 'O Mantuan soul, the soul of courtesy, / Whose glory is still current in the world' (*Inferno* II 58–60). Ovid had concluded the *Metamorphoses*, which Dante knew as well as he did the *Aeneid*, with the words: 'If truth at all / Is stablished by poetic prophecy, / My fame shall live to all eternity'.[3]

With these thoughts in mind, Dante found it impossible to believe that the great poets of Antiquity, because of their blameless ignorance of a Christianity which was unavailable to them, could not be touched by the grace of the Christian God. Hence his inspired creation, in Limbo just outside the bounds of Hell proper, of the Noble Castle, the tranquil home of

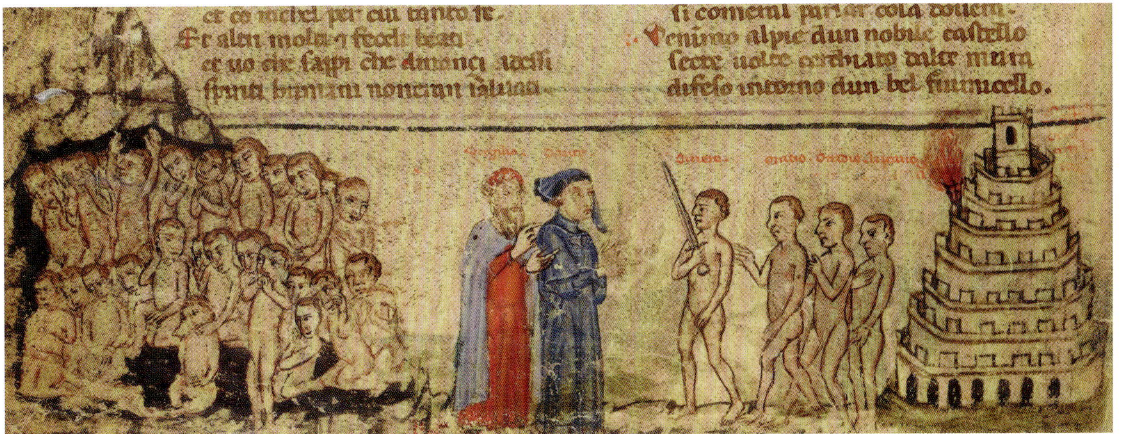

Fig. 2 Virgil and Dante meet the Poets of the Noble Castle (*Inferno* IV), 1350–75. Bodleian Libraries, University of Oxford, MS. Holkham misc. 48, p. 6.

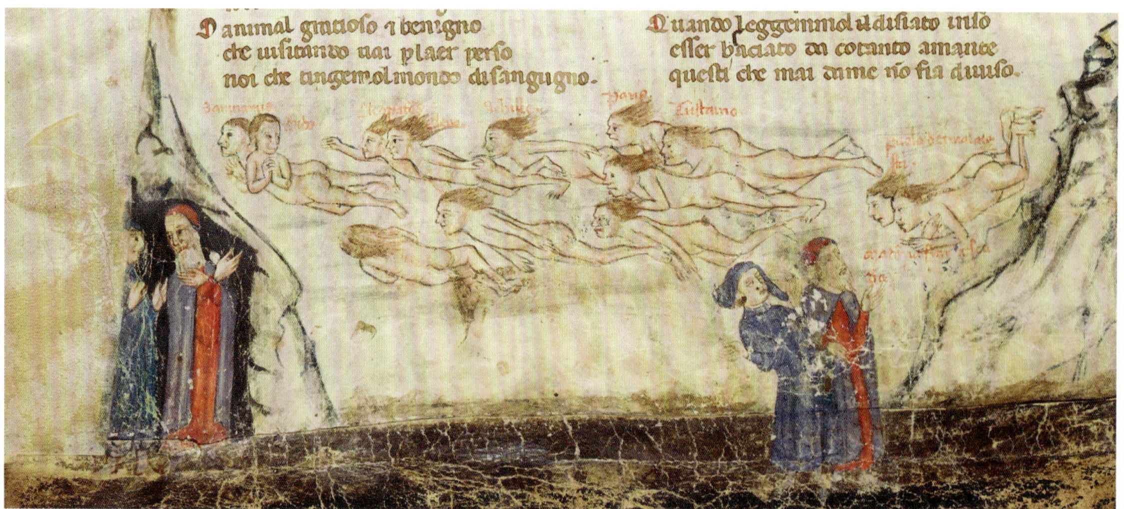

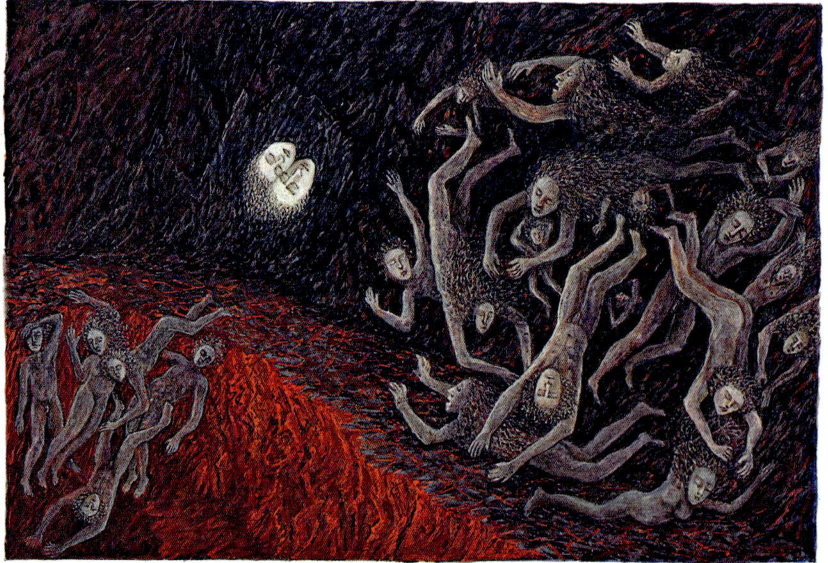

Above:
Fig. 3 Dante and Virgil encounter Paolo and Francesca (*Inferno* v), 1350–75. Bodleian Libraries, University of Oxford, MS. Holkham misc. 48, p. 8.

Left:
Fig. 4 Monika Beisner (b. 1942), Paolo and Francesca (*Inferno* v), 2001. With the artist's permission.

the ancient poets and other sages. When the pilgrim Dante asks Virgil to explain this arrangement, he is told that their virtuous reputation in the world has earned them this privilege as a divine grace: 'Their honourable name, / Still echoing throughout the world above, / Wins grace in heaven and thus advances them' (*Inferno* iv 76–78) (fig. 2).

As the reader follows the pilgrim Dante on his journey through the other world, it turns out that the entire *Comedy* is a vast hall of fame, in which a host of characters, ranging from the most eminent to the very obscure, are commemorated and made famous by Dante's poetry. The adulterous lovers Paolo and Francesca, tossed in the perpetual wind of the fifth circle of Hell with those who yielded to passion (*Inferno* v) (figs 3, 4); Bertran de Born, the troubadour poet who stirred up civil war within the family of King Henry II of England, and who appropriately carries his own severed head 'just like a lantern' (*Inferno* xxviii) (fig. 5); and many others who would otherwise remain unknown to us, live on through the lines of the *Comedy*. In vividly evoked encounters in the course of the journey, the reader comes to believe completely in these personalities. Scholars have been able to verify the historical existence of Dante's army of characters; but in every case their presentation to us is moulded by the artist. We overlook the artifice, and we are distracted from the poet Dante's responsibility for the creation of their fame by the realism of the writing and also by the internal morality of the poem, in the course of which the pilgrim called Dante – and the

Fig. 5 Gustave Doré (1832–1883), The Sowers of Discord: Bertran de Born (*Inferno* xxviii). *Dante's Inferno with English text by Cary, illustrated by G. Doré* (London, 1866). Private Collection.

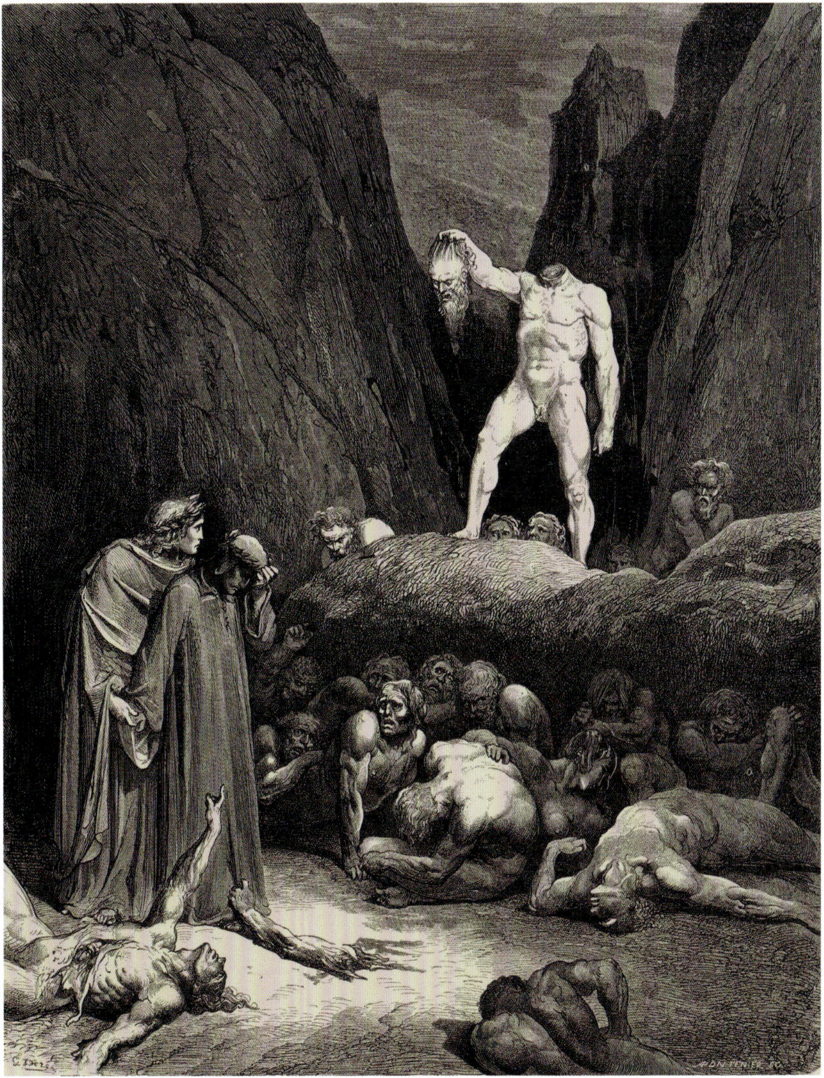

reader – are educated to recognise the emptiness of worldly honour in the absence of divine grace.

The one thing which preoccupies all the ghostly figures Dante encounters in Hell is the state of their reputation on earth: this futile concern is all that remains to them. Characteristic is the gluttonous Ciacco, who though condemned for eternity to the stinking morass of the third circle under continuous rain and hail, is still moved to urge Dante to remind his fellow Florentines of him on his return (*Inferno* VI 89). As he falls back into the mud, we realise that the natural condition of Hell is, in fact, silence; that the only reason we hear of the souls there is that the poet Dante has spoken for them. The suicide Pier della Vigna is persuaded to tell his tale when Virgil assures him that Dante, when he returns to Italy, will be able to 'Restore you to your worldly reputation' (*Inferno* XIII 53). In the burning sands of the sodomites, Dante meets three other Florentines who expect that he will recognise them because of their 'fame' (*Inferno* XVI 31). Dante is not displeased to see them, but the good reputation which they enjoyed as honourable citizens has not sufficed to earn them salvation; and the pilgrim passes on. In the lower depths of Hell, where the worst offences are punished, the sinners are reluctant to identify themselves for fear Dante may worsen their image in the world. The thief Vanni Fucci, who robbed a church and laid the blame on others, declares that he is more tormented than at his own death by being recognised and made to tell his story to Dante (*Inferno* XXIV 133–35). Guido da Montefeltro, among the false counsellors, is only prepared to speak of his deathly advice to the pope because he cannot believe that his interlocutor will return to the world (*Inferno* XXVII 61–66). Wedged in the perpetual ice of the traitors in Cocytus, Count Ugolino hopes, by telling his story to Dante, that his enemy's 'infamy' in the world may be increased (*Inferno* XXXIII 8).

So even while the pilgrim in the vision – who is, at the same time, the reader – is made to understand that the fixation with fame and reputation shared by everyone in Hell is sterile, Dante the poet conjures into our enduring memories – seven centuries on – the undying images of those same sinners. Dante has it both ways, and he continues to do so in the higher realms of the other world. On the mountain of Purgatory the lowest and weightiest of the sins being purged is that of pride. The sinners are bowed low under the weight of great rocks which, in expiation of the offence of which they have repented, they willingly carry until the due time for their release. One of these is the illuminator of manuscripts Oderisi da Gubbio, who has put behind him the pride he once took in his reputation. 'Vanity of vanities is man's renown!' he exclaims, going on to moralise about vainglory: 'A changing gust of wind is worldly fame, / Now here, now there – and what we call it varies / According to the quarter it blows from' (*Purgatorio* XI 100–102). The subject is an especially poignant one

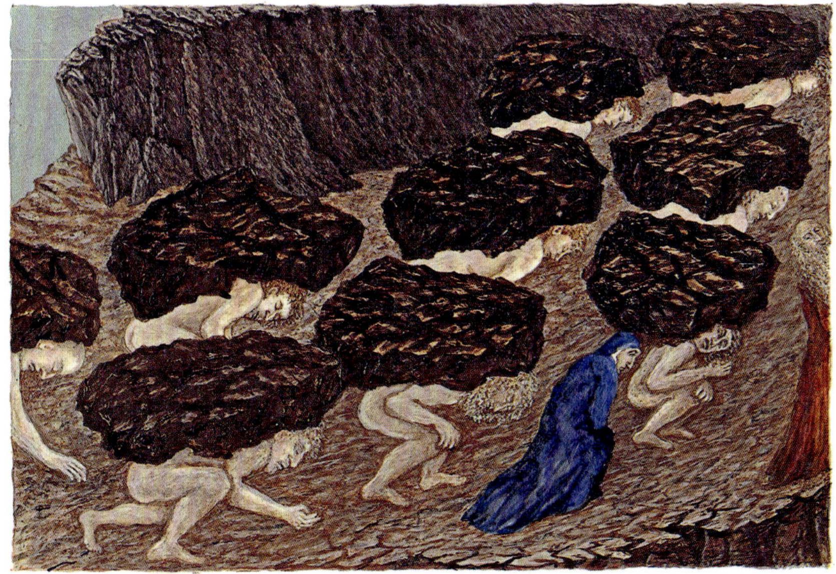

Fig. 6 Monika Beisner (b. 1942), Dante and Oderisi in the Circle of the Proud (*Purgatorio* XI), 2001. With the artist's permission.

for illustrators of the *Comedy*, including Monika Beisner, whose images, a microscopic and painstaking labour completed over a seven-year period for an edition of the *Comedy* published in 2001, show the influence of medieval illuminators of the poem (fig. 6).

Worldly glory is transient: the message seems clear. Yet in the line immediately preceding this warning, Oderisi, referring to the poets Guido Guinizelli and Guido Cavalcanti, older contemporaries of and significant influences on Dante, has just prophesied that 'now perhaps / There's one who'll drive them both out of the nest': an unequivocal allusion to the coming fame of Dante himself. In *Paradiso* Dante continues without embarrassment to invoke the Muse of poetry, 'who make[s] great minds / Illustrious, and render[s] them immortal' (*Paradiso* XVIII 82–83). There is no doubt of Dante's self-awareness of his place in a lineage of great poets, as he indicated at the outset of the *Comedy* when the five noble poets and seers of Antiquity, residents of the Noble Castle, 'invited me to join their circle: / I was the sixth, with such great minds as they' (*Inferno* IV 101–2; see fig. 2). Yet from a Christian perspective Dante saw his status and responsibility as even greater than this, describing himself as the 'scribe' of a divine vision (*Paradiso* X 27), just like John witnessing the Apocalypse on the island of Patmos.

In Dante's eyes, the right kind of fame can in fact do good in the world. So it is with the troubadour poet and later Cistercian monk, Folco of Marseille, encountered in Paradise. Folco is first pointed out, in the heavenly circle of Venus, by another soul who says of him that he still enjoys 'great fame' in the world, and will continue to do so for another five centuries. The same soul asks a rhetorical question: 'So should not men seek excellence / Until a second life [after death] succeeds the first?' (*Paradiso* IX 39–42). And in the heaven of Mars, the poet's own ancestor, Cacciaguida, foretells that 's'infutura la tua vita' ('your life will last out') far beyond even the punishment in Hell which would be imposed on his fellow-Florentines who, in a factional *coup d'état*, had vindictively exiled him (*Paradiso* XVII 98–9). So often does he return to the subject that it is clear that Dante was anything but indifferent to fame.

Indeed, in Dante's eyes the worst thing of all was to have failed to act in the world or sought fame of any sort. When he and Virgil have just entered the gate of Hell, passing beneath the terrible inscription 'Abandon hope, all you who enter here', but have not yet fully arrived in the infernal kingdom, Dante's ears are assaulted by

> Deformed and diverse tongues, terrible sounds,
> Words venting misery, outbursts of rage,
> Loud voices, soft ones, sounds of slapping hands …

He then discerns in the unlit landscape an anonymous, infinite troupe, running in an endless and futile circle (fig. 7). He learns from Virgil that these were people who had done nothing while on earth: 'the lives they lived were such / They earned no infamy, and earned no praise'. Their sounds

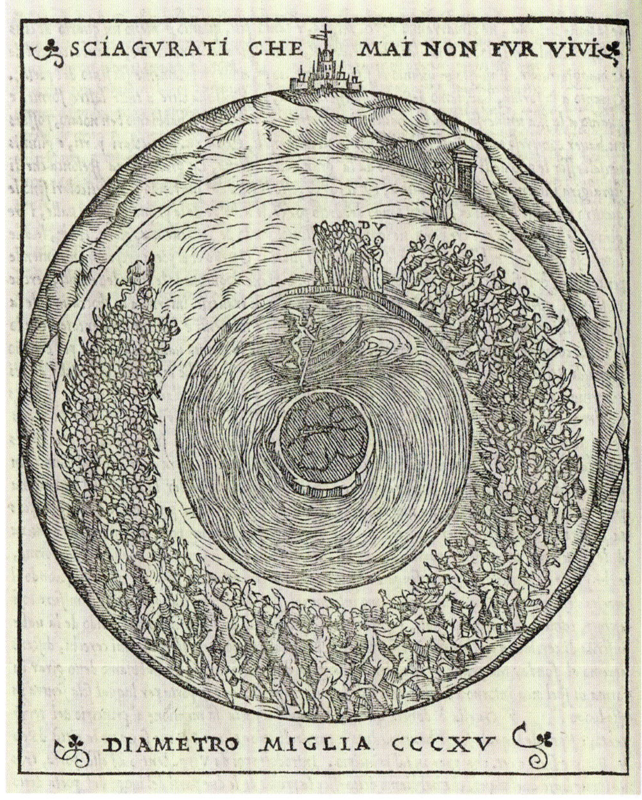

Fig. 7 The punishment of 'those who never were alive'. *La comedia di Dante Aligieri con la noua espositione di Alessandro Vellutello* (Venice, 1544). Bodleian Libraries, University of Oxford, Taylor Institution Library, ARCH.8.It.1544(2).

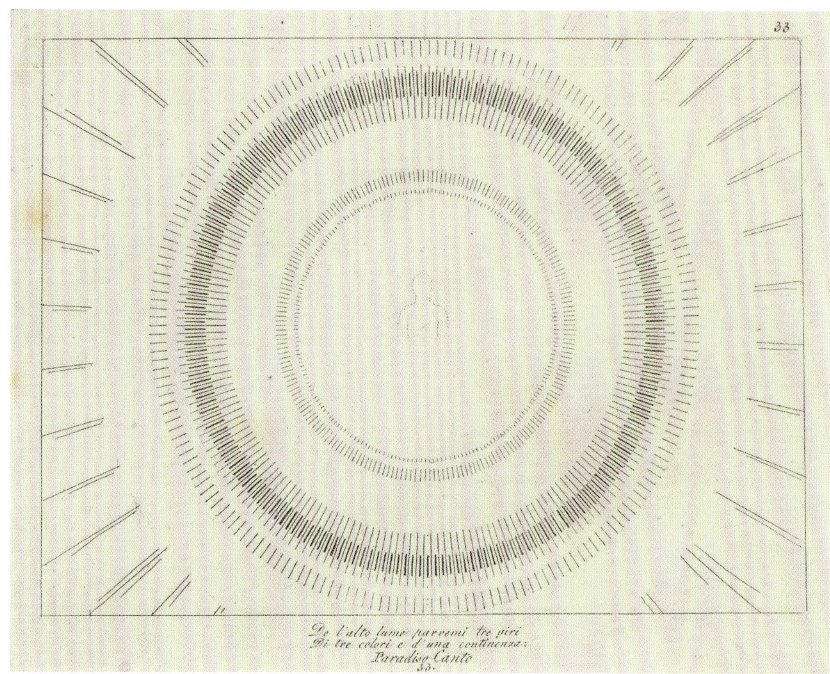

Fig. 8 John Flaxman (1755–1826), The Light Supreme (*Paradiso* XXXIII). *La Divina comedia di Dante Alighieri … compost da Giovanni Flaxman* (Amsterdam, 1793). Bodleian Libraries, University of Oxford, Vet.B5 d.61.

are provoked by frustration, for having never really lived on earth ('mai non fur' vivi'), in eternity they cannot die. Denied the notoriety of either good or evil, 'The world accords them not the least renown'. Virgil's comment is terse: 'Enough of this – you've seen them, now pass on' (*Inferno* III 25–51).

Dante condemned those caught up in the solipsistic pursuit of mere worldly celebrity, even while he perpetuated the names of arch-examples; but he reconfigured fame to become a means of salvation: his own and that of others. The notion of fame itself was old, but his particular combination of Roman glory and Christian morality was distinctive, striking a balance between this-worldly and transcendent aims which would resonate far into the future. Moreover, his radically inclusive vision of human community meant that, in place of the narrow elites of pagan heroes and Christian martyrs conventionally held up as examples of good living, the *Comedy* presented an infinitely diverse cast of women and men, each realised by the poet in their unique individuality. When the pilgrim, at the final climax of his vision, sees the Holy Trinity in the form of three concentric circles of light, he also recognises within that circling light a reflection, 'come lume reflesso…pinta della nostra effige' ('a light that was reflected…painted with the Image of Mankind': an allusion both to the incarnate Christ and to humanity made in God's image) (*Paradiso* XXXIII 131) (fig. 8). In that moment, the visionary realises that humankind in general, and each distinct individual, is a glorious embodiment of divinity, and truly deserving of the lasting fame which only the poet can convey.

THE IMAGE OF THE POET

Fame on earth has always been bound up with a visual image: we need to know what our saints and heroes look like. The idea of Dante has been shaped from the start by representations of him. Each age, just as it re-reads the *Comedy*, at the same time re-envisions its author. Readers always believe they know what Dante looked like, which is a remarkable claim to authentic connection, considering how little information we really have. The story of the quest for Dante's image is testimony to a deep human longing.

It was the Renaissance painter Raphael, revolutionary creator of portraits, who crystallised what would prove to be the most enduring visual image of Dante. The artist had seen depictions by Florentine painters, of which the prominent tribute painted by Domenico di Michelino for the cathedral on the anniversary of Dante's birth in 1465, a panel from the workshop of Botticelli and a fresco by Signorelli are surviving examples (frontispiece; figs 9, 1), that had established a more-or-less canonical image: these lie behind Raphael's version, painted around 1510 in the public apartments of the papal palace of the Vatican in Rome.

Characterised by its jutting chin, hooked nose and piercing stare, the daunting face recalls older images of biblical prophets and classical philosophers. These lofty connotations were reinforced by Raphael's situation of the poet in the Vatican frescoes both amongst the imaginative geniuses of Mount Parnassus and in the company of the Church Fathers and other theologians engaged in discussion of the Incarnation of Christ. Later artists would copy these representations of the poet, especially the latter, which is closer to the eye level of the visitor (figs 10, 11). Raphael's version was canonised by its use for the first appearance of Dante on the title-page of an edition of his works, in 1564 (fig. 12).

Fame is always, in some sense, political. The figure of Dante in the sixteenth century was recruited to the service of the new Medici principality of Tuscany. Long gone, by this point, was the hostility which had caused the poet's exile in 1302. However, differing inspiration was to be found in Dante according to political taste: whereas Florentine republicans of the later Middle Ages – and Italian nationalists in the nineteenth century – appreciated his condemnation of tyrants and emphasis on solidarity, the Medici princes of the sixteenth century promoted his image as the cultural icon of a centralised regime. In a highly charged group portrait of 1544, the painter and Medici propagandist Giorgio Vasari constructed an idea of civilisation as a canon of great Tuscan poets, presided over by Dante (fig. 13).

Dante holds up a volume of Virgil to his contemporary Guido Cavalcanti, while his other hand is poised authoritatively over the terrestrial and celestial globes, indicative of his understanding both of earth and Heaven. To

Fig. 9 Workshop of Sandro Botticelli (1444/5–1510), Portrait of Dante, c.1480. Oil on canvas. Bodmer Collection, Geneva. © Bridgeman Images.

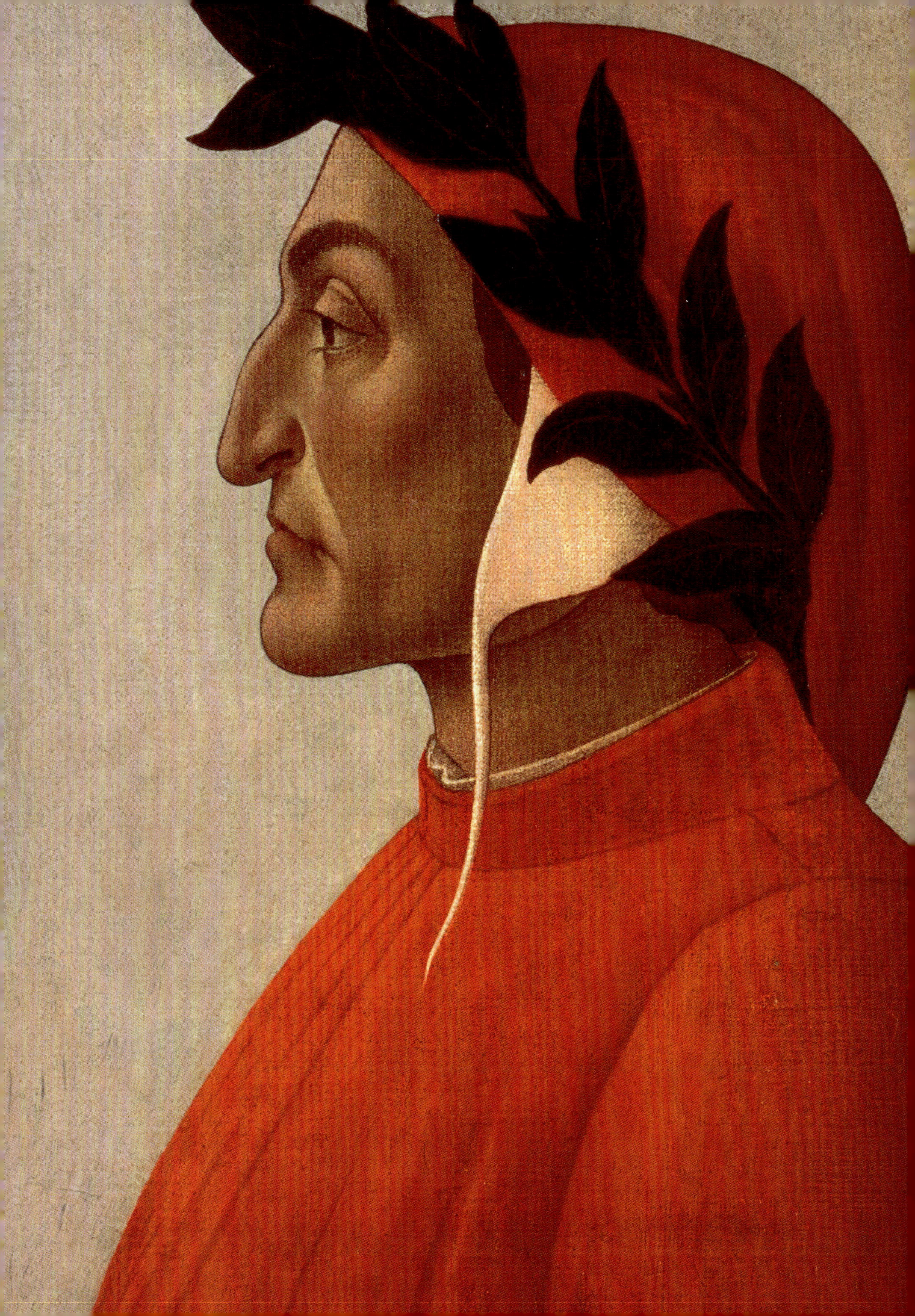

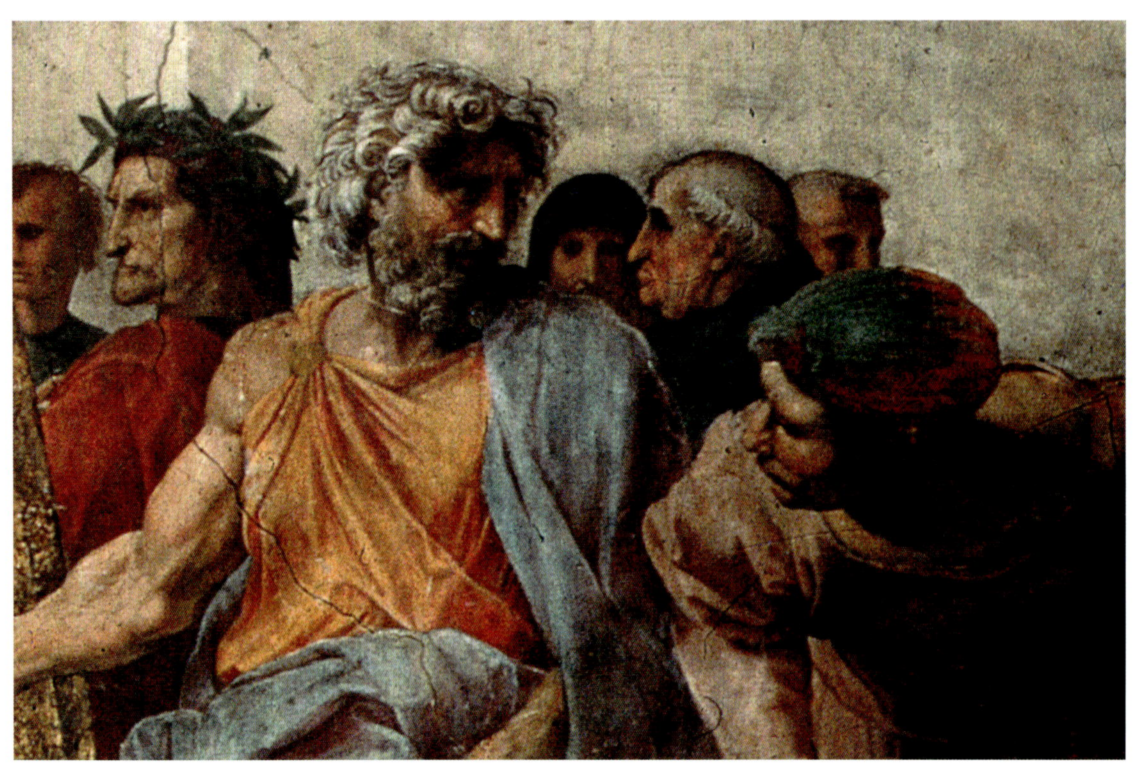

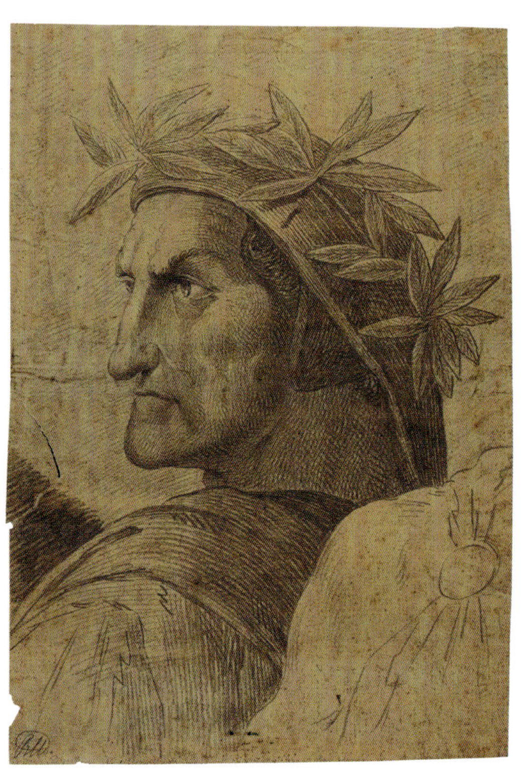

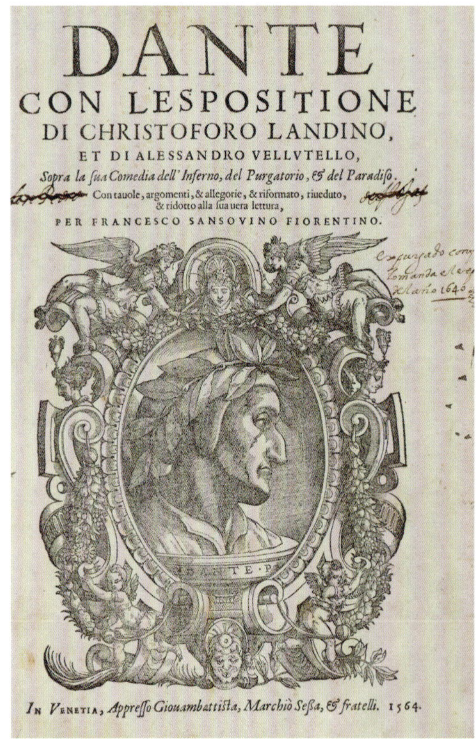

DANTE
CON LESPOSITIONE
DI CHRISTOFORO LANDINO,
ET DI ALESSANDRO VELLVTELLO,
Sopra la sua Comedia dell' Inferno, del Purgatorio, & del Paradiso.
Con tauole, argomenti, & allegorie, & riformato, riueduto,
& ridotto alla sua uera lettura,
PER FRANCESCO SANSOVINO FIORENTINO.

In Venetia, Appresso Giouambattista, Marchiò Sessa, & fratelli. 1564.

Opposite top:
Fig. 10 Raphael, *Disputa*, Stanza della Segnatura, Vatican Palace, Rome (detail), Dante among the theologians. Photo © Alinari / Bridgeman Images

Opposite bottom left:
Fig. 11 Possibly by a follower of Thomas Lawrence (1769–1830), *Head of Dante, after Raphael*, *c.*1800–30. Black chalk on yellowish paper, 40.2 × 28.5 cm. Ashmolean Museum (WA1863.1413). © Ashmolean Museum, University of Oxford.

Opposite bottom right:
Fig. 12 *Dante con l'espositione di Christoforo Landino et di Alessandro Vellutello sopra la sua comedia* (Venice, 1564). Bodleian Libraries, University of Oxford, Taylor Institution Library ARCH.Fol.It.1564(1).

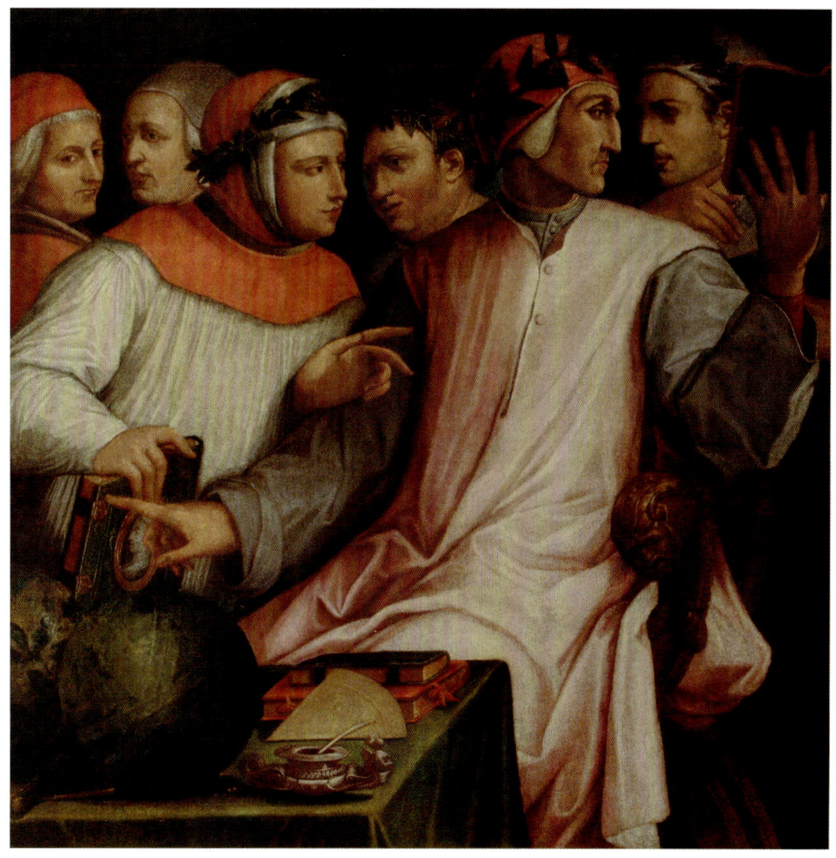

Right:
Fig. 13 Workshop of Giorgio Vasari (1511–1574), *Six Tuscan Poets*. Oil painting on canvas, 121.9 × 121.9 cm, 1544. Oriel College, Oxford. By permission of the Provost and Fellows of Oriel College.

Dante's right, Petrarch (1304–74), scholar of antiquity and vernacular love poet, presses forward in his clerical robes. Behind in the centre, the writer Boccaccio (1313–75), who gave the first public lectures on the *Comedy*, looks over the others' shoulders. The remaining figures are probably Cino da Pistoia and Guittone d'Arezzo, fellow poets of Dante's youth who were involved with him in the creation of the *dolce stil nuovo*, the 'sweet new style' of Dante's early love poems. Created for the Medicean governor of Pisa and Dante scholar Luca Martini, Vasari's composite portrait of poetic genius helped to present the new regime as a vehicle of the noblest creative art. This image of the Dantesque foundations of not merely Tuscan but European culture has proved enduring. By Vasari's own account, the work was much copied: a version now in the Minneapolis Art Institute may be the prototype, while a second, owned by Oriel College in Oxford, is also of high quality and was probably made in Vasari's workshop. The work also circulated as an engraving.

In the nineteenth century a surge of Romantic interest in Dante as a medieval visionary and poet of love called for a new visual icon, which was conveniently revealed by a dramatic intervention in a Florentine palace. Not many years after Dante's death, it was said in Florence that his portrait

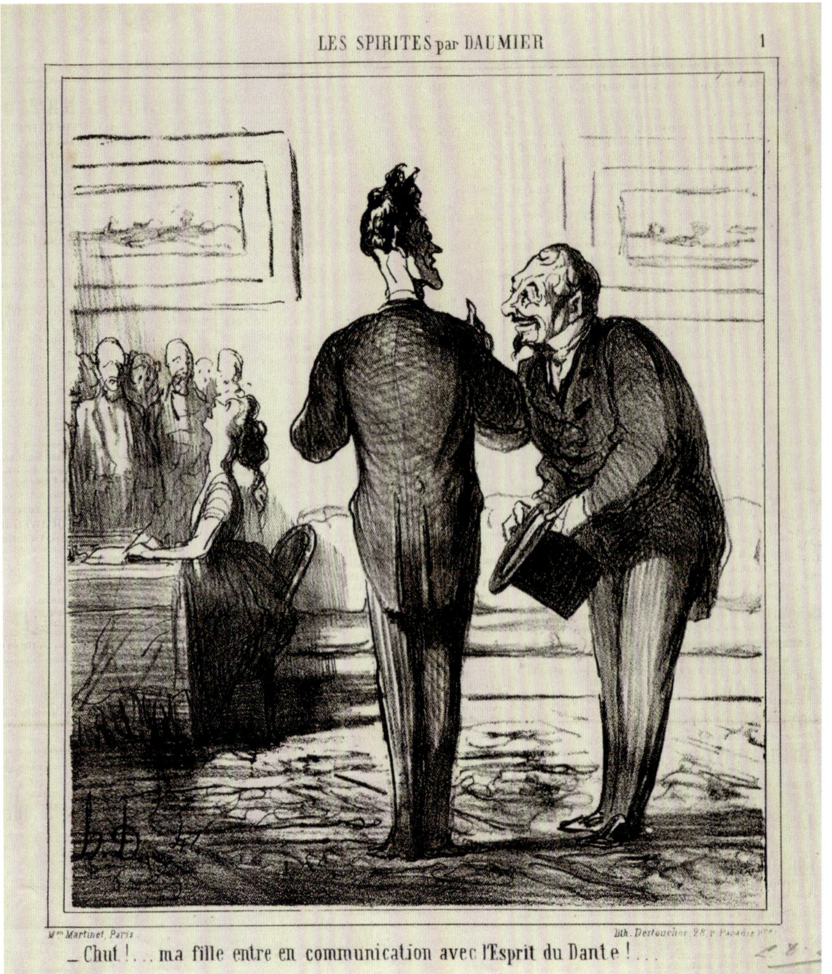

Fig. 14 Honoré Daumier (1808–1879), 'Hush! My daughter is entering into communication with the spirit of Dante'. Lithograph for *Le Charivari*, published 4 November 1865. Private Collection.

had been included by none other than the celebrated painter Giotto in a series of frescoes in the chapel of the Palazzo del Podestà, or Bargello. Such stories were symptomatic of the early cult of the poet in the city from which, ironically, he had spent the last two decades of his life in exile. In 1840 Seymour Kirkup, a highly eccentric English Dante enthusiast, long resident in Florence, had the whitewash in this chapel stripped back in the anticipation of finding an authentic representation of Dante which would also link two great artists in an iconic Florentine building. In his mysterious house at the south end of the old Arno bridge, Kirkup had visions of the poet, and came to believe that his daughter could speak directly with Dante and record his messages. Many at this time believed in the possibility of communication with the dead, providing a new stage for famous characters of history: a mid-nineteenth-century cartoon by the French caricaturist Daumier – produced as a satire for his own times, at a moment of revived fascination with the psychic – alludes to Kirkup's séances (fig. 14). On the basis of a tracing of the rediscovered fresco supposed (probably wrongly) to represent Dante, Kirkup had a reproduction made, which would fix the image of the lovelorn poet for a new generation of Romantic readers (fig. 15).

The image played well to growing interest in Dante's youthful love poetry and his relationship with Beatrice. The first complete English translation of Dante's *Vita Nuova* or *The New Life*, a poetic account of his love which ends tragically following the death of Beatrice at the age of twenty-four, was published in Florence in 1846. The newly circulating picture of Dante, young and hopeful, was also an inspiration to those campaigning for the liberation of Italy from Austrian domination, and Kirkup sent a copy of

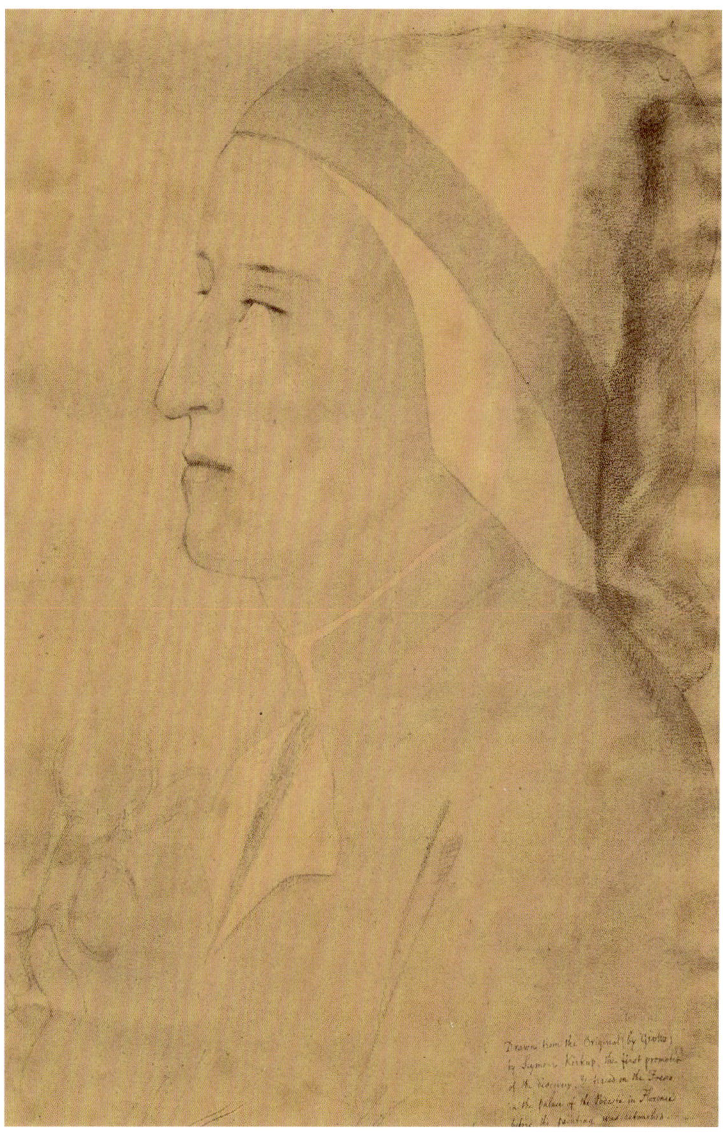

Fig. 15 'Dante'. Chromolithograph, printed for the Arundel Society, 1859. Made from a copy by Seymour Kirkup of the Bargello portrait rediscovered in 1840. Bodleian Library, University of Oxford, LP795.

his drawing of the 'Dante' fresco to the passionate nationalist Gabriele Rossetti, then living with other Italian exiles in London. Rossetti's son, Dante Gabriel, had not at first taken much interest in the figure after whom he was named; but this drawing was the catalyst of a lifelong fascination. In 1852 he completed a watercolour depicting the story of the painting of Dante's portrait by Giotto (fig. 16). In a later version Rossetti portrayed himself as the artist (fig. 17). Out of his growing identification with both of these distinguished predecessors, Rossetti developed in addition a consciousness of his role in promoting the revival of their fame in his own day. He believed this could redeem the fallen world. Rossetti was among critics of contemporary materialism who had faith in art as a means to spiritualise ordinary existence. Through emulation of Dante and Beatrice, as they appeared in the *Vita Nuova*, Rossetti hoped that his own world might be given a 'new life'.

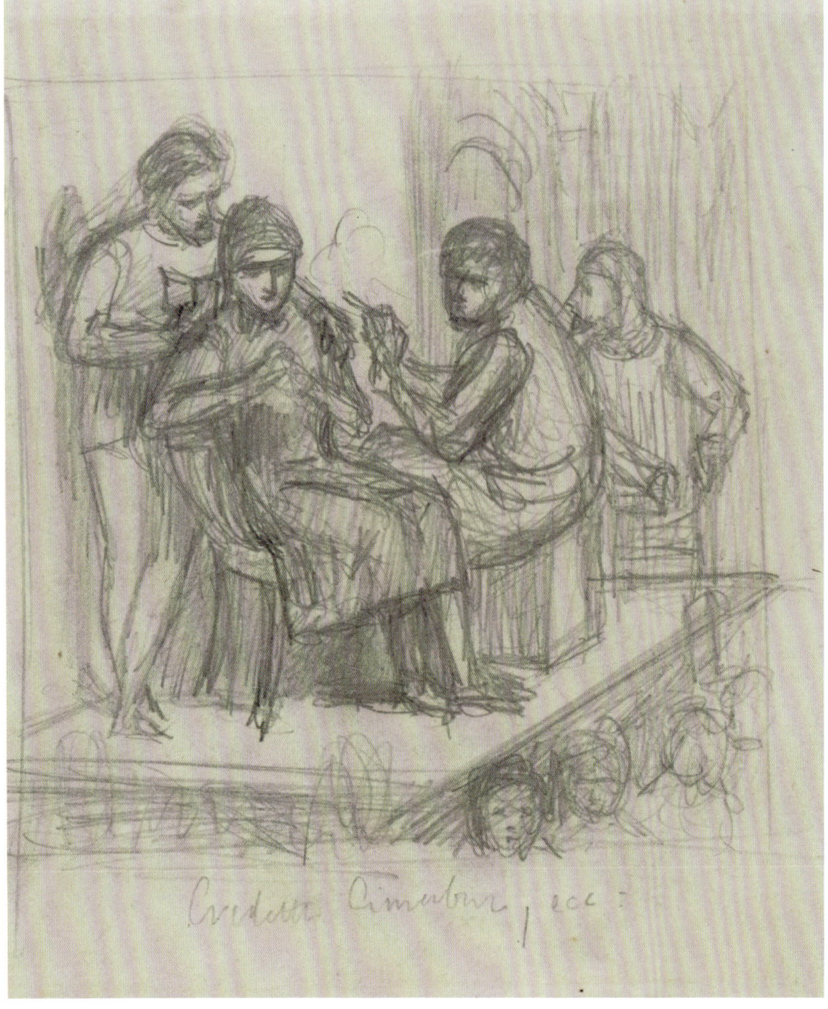

Fig. 16 Dante Gabriel Rossetti (1828–82), *Study for 'Giotto Painting the Portrait of Dante'*, *c.*1852. Graphite on wove paper, 12 × 12 cm. Ashmolean Museum (WA2014.36). © Ashmolean Museum, University of Oxford.

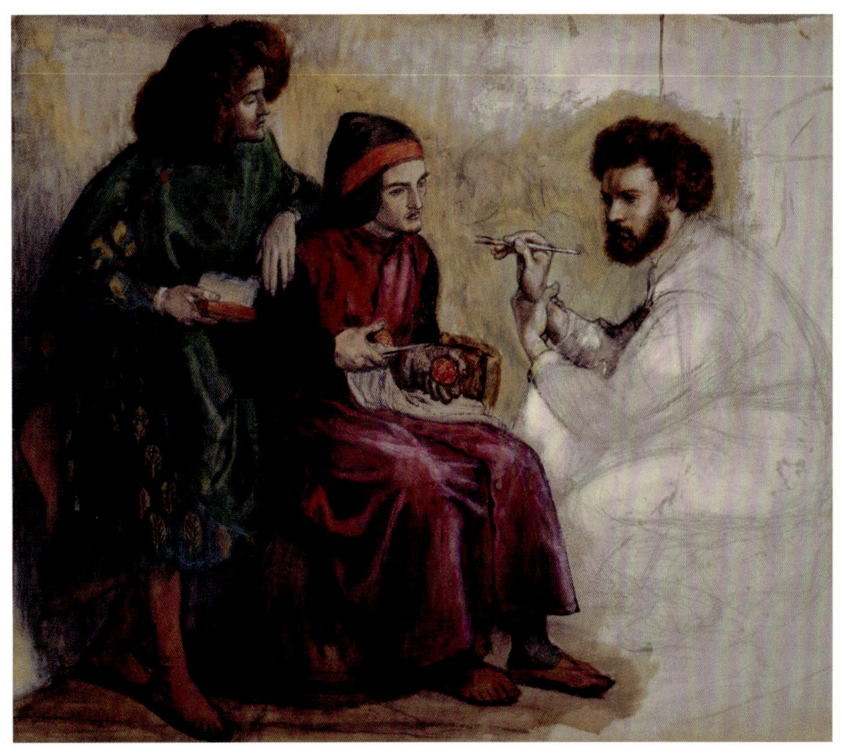

Fig. 17 Dante Gabriel Rossetti (1828–1882), *Giotto Painting the Portrait of Dante*. Watercolour, gouache and graphite, 47.6 × 56.4 cm, *c*.1859. Harvard Art Museums/Fogg Museum, Bequest of Grenville L. Winthrop.

In this context the figure of Beatrice herself attracted growing interest, not merely as Dante's muse but as a model of feminine inspiration and authority in her own right. The celebration of Beatrice reached a climax in the Beatrice exhibition held in Florence in 1890. Initiated by the opera composer Carlotta Ferrari, this vast project was a largely female undertaking, and was presented as a demonstration of the prominent role of women in the economy and culture of the recently founded Italian state. The programme included *tableaux vivants* based on the *Vita Nuova*, musical compositions by women, 10,000 books written by women in the thirty years since the creation of Italy, displays of women's vital work in the textile industries, and hundreds of paintings, sculptures and ceramics by female artists. A commemorative medal designed by Luigi Gori glorified Beatrice with an inscription taken from *Paradiso* XXIII: 'O Beatrice, dolce guida e cara!' ('O Beatrice, my sweet and loving guide!') (fig. 18).

Fig. 18 Commemorative medal from the 'Beatrice' exhibition held in Florence in May–June 1890. Bronze, designed by Luigi Gori. Private Collection.

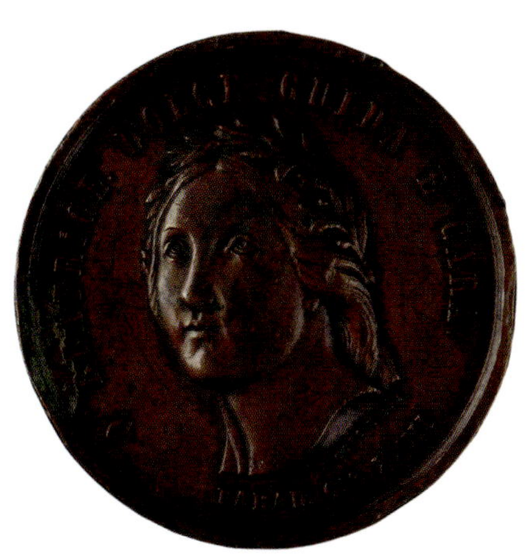

In addition to the supposedly authentic portrait and the living voice of Dante, Seymour Kirkup was the probable originator of a no less wonderful supposed relic of the poet: his 'death-mask'. This marvellous object Kirkup said he had received (in exchange for a King Charles spaniel) from Lorenzo Bartolini, a renowned nineteenth-century Florentine maker

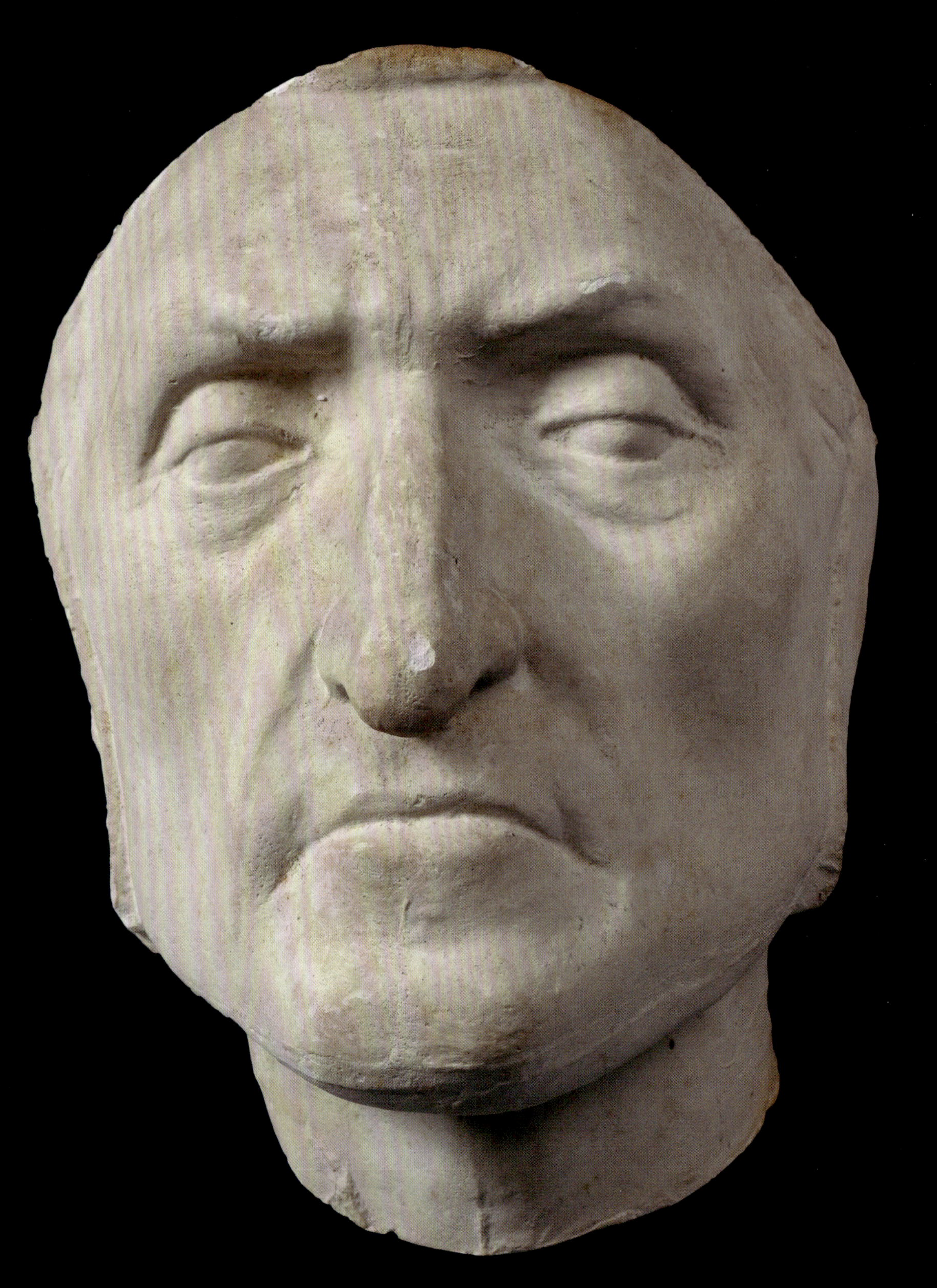

Opposite:
Fig. 19 'Death-mask of Dante', presented to the Oxford Dante Society by Seymour Kirkup. Plaster, 19th century. Bodleian Libraries, University of Oxford, LP 900.

Right:
Fig. 20 Mask of Dante Alighieri, Italian, 19th century. Plaster of Paris, mounted on wooden plaque, approx. 22 cm. Ashmolean Museum (WA1916.76). © Ashmolean Museum, University of Oxford.

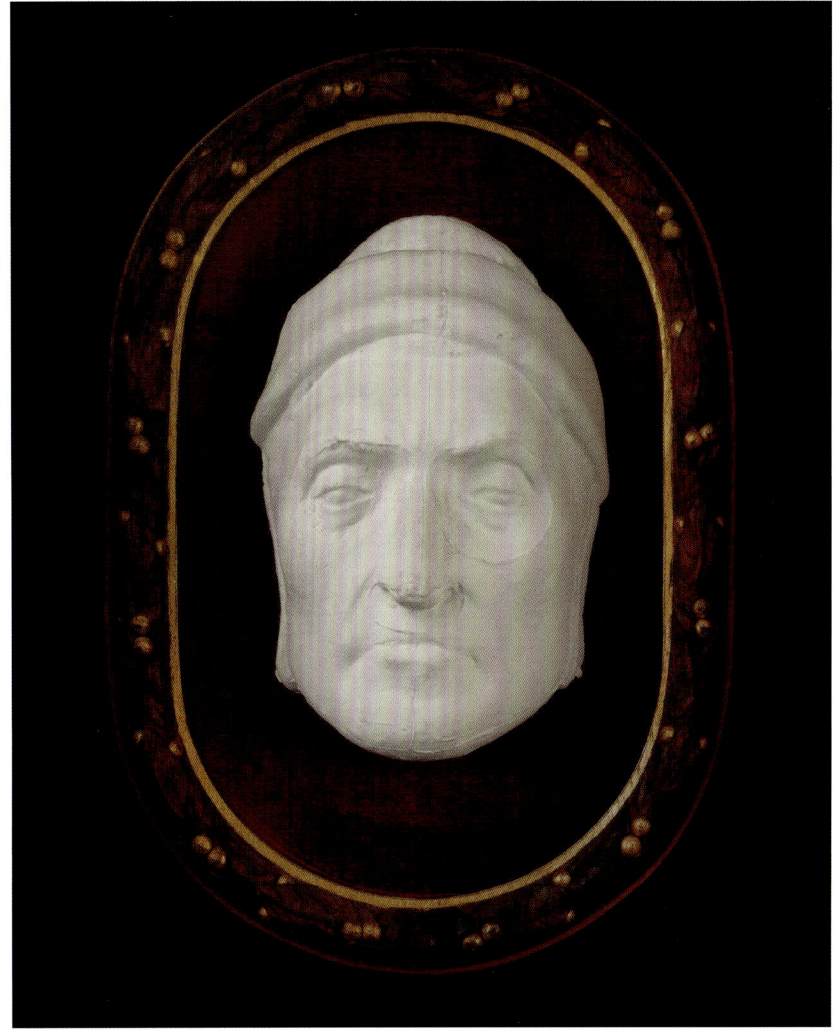

of plaster casts. There was, in truth, no death-mask of Dante. Bartolini is likely to have taken his impression, perhaps at Kirkup's suggestion, from a (now lost) late-fifteenth-century carved portrait on the tomb of Dante at Ravenna (itself said erroneously to have been derived from a death-mask). But the Romantic period generated so strong a desire for the sense of a real encounter with the poet that disbelief was suspended. Kirkup's mask passed indirectly to the Palazzo Vecchio in Florence, where it remains as a sacred treasure, but he also distributed a number of copies, in 1879 presenting one to the recently founded Oxford Dante Society (fig. 19).

A second 'mask of Dante', which probably came to Oxford in the same period, derives from a different source: a terracotta bust of the poet in the Palazzo del Nero in Florence, which in the nineteenth century was itself believed to have been made from a cast taken at the time of Dante's death (fig. 20). As has often been noticed about the modern cult of celebrity, this retains strong echoes of the medieval and later Catholic veneration of the material relics of the saints. The quasi-religious desire to see the true face of Dante Alighieri is a striking manifestation of this: it bears in particular a close analogy to the history of the wish to see the face of Christ.

The cult of the material and imagined body of Dante was to reach its apogee with the sensational rediscovery of his bones. On his death at Ravenna on 14 September 1321, Dante's body was buried in the Franciscan church. Towards the end of the following century, the tomb was re-framed in a temple-like shrine, at the initiative of the humanist and Venetian governor of Ravenna, Bernardo Bembo. Attempts by Florentines to secure the bones for his native city were frustrated by their removal to a secret location. In 1865, the sixth centenary of Dante's birth, restoration work fortuitously revealed a box identified – convincingly – as containing the bones of the poet (largely complete, although missing the mandible from the skull). The event was announced as a 'miracle', and reverential pilgrims processed in their thousands to the tomb of the figure now identified as the secular patron saint of the new Italian state, created just four years earlier. The sacred status of this site would be formalised from 1936 by the creation, in the area around the tomb, of the 'Zona del Silenzio' which still marks out this area of Ravenna.

The box containing Dante's bones was opened again in 1921, on the sixth centenary of his death. Fabio Frassetto, a young anthropologist, was determined to use the bones to reconstruct the face of the poet, despite official fears that this would trivialise its venerable subject. Revealing the nationalist and racial preoccupations of the period, Frassetto insisted that his research (which he also claimed was authorised by Dante himself in a spiritualist meeting with the poet at Trieste in 1929) showed the 'strong and virile' Dante to have been not (as some had claimed) of the Arian but 'of the Mediterranean race'. The Fascist connotations of this racial language, which at this time was coming increasingly to the fore in Germany but also in Italy, are evident. Frassetto planned a film, never completed, which presented the head of Dante as embodying the essence of Italian culture. The bust moulded under his direction was indeed widely disseminated and still presides in many schoolrooms, libraries and university halls around the world (fig. 21). Federico Fellini, who saw as a child the film, *Inferno*, mentioned below, and acknowledged the profound influence of Dante on his own films, remembered from his schooldays the way in which that bust, with its 'severe face of a judge or a spy', appeared to act as a figure of surveillance.

In 2006 anthropologists at the University of Bologna, using the data collected by Frassetto and new methods of facial reconstruction, made what *La Repubblica* sensationally announced on its front page to be 'the true

Fig. 21 Alfonso Borghesani (1882–1964), bust of Dante based on measurements provided by Fabio Frassetto, 1938. Image and copyright Fototeca Zeri Bologna.

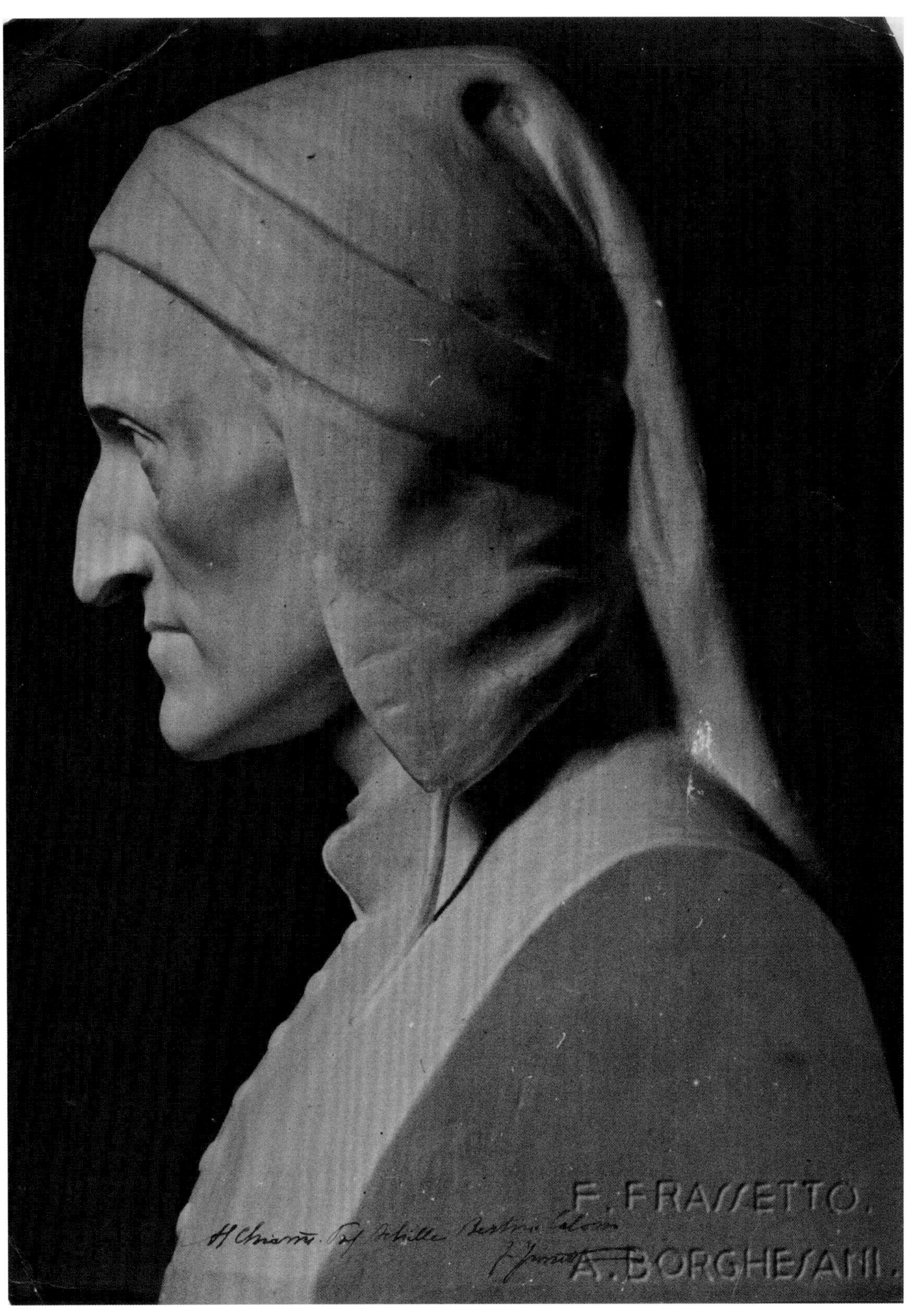
F. FRASSETTO.
A. BORGHESANI.

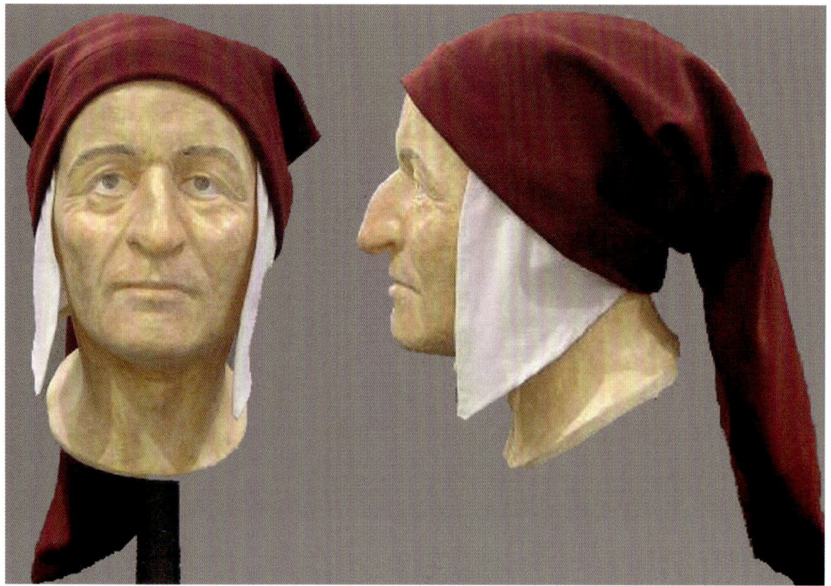

Fig. 22 Reconstruction of Dante's face using forensic anthropology techniques, 2006. Work and photograph by Giorgio Gruppioni. Reproduced with permission.

– gentle – face of Dante' (fig. 22). The makers themselves were more qualified in their claims, but the press had a strong vested interest in promoting the idea of its tangibility and truth status, as well as its immediacy. While Frassetto's bust had been influenced by historic images of the poet as a sunken-eyed, hook-nosed prophet, this most recent reconstruction makes Dante rather less exceptional: he is Everyman. Perhaps this is the desired image of Dante for the new millennium. In September 2021 the bones will once more be exposed, when the occasion is certain to generate fresh debate surrounding the supposed appearance of the poet.

The only relatively early description of Dante, which can be set alongside the skeletal evidence and the various myths surrounding what he looked like, is the testimony of Boccaccio, who was too young to have known Dante but who talked in Ravenna with people who had known the poet in his fifties:

> Our poet was of middle height and in his later years he walked somewhat bent over, with a grave and gentle gait. He was clad always in the most seemly attire, such as befitted his ripe years. His face was long, his nose aquiline, and his eyes rather big than small. His jaws were large, and his lower lip protruded. His complexion was dark, his hair and beard thick, black and curly, and his expression ever melancholy and thoughtful.[4]

Dante's historical appearance is largely lost to us. But this will never suppress the conviction that if we were to meet him, we should know him at once.

THE MIRROR OF FAME: IN DANTE'S COMPANY

Dante's enormous celebrity, which reached a peak of Dantemania around 1900 but which continues in different forms today, has made him a touchstone for the fame of others. To be seen in his company became a mark of distinction. What was true for individual celebrities was valid also for places. Dante's native Florence and the cities of his exile are peppered with public inscriptions of passages from the *Comedy* with local reference, by virtue of which the location claims honourable status by association. Even Oxford, which Dante never visited, brushed up a legend of the poet's presence to add lustre to the city's name. Max Beerbohm gently ironised this idea, showing the university proctor's failure to recognise the distinguished visitor wandering Oxford's streets by night (fig. 23).

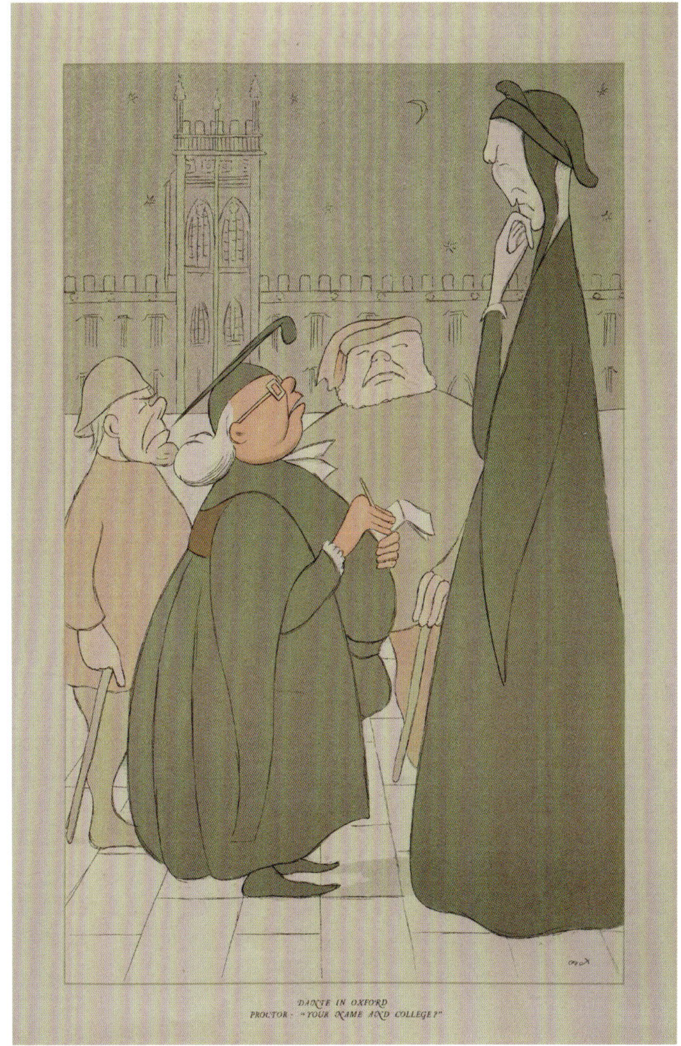

Fig. 23 Sir Max Beerbohm (1872–1956), 'Dante in Oxford', illustration from *The Poets' Corner*, William Heinemann: London, 1904. Lithograph, 37 × 28 cm. Ashmolean Museum, University of Oxford, Western Art Print Room, Hope Collection XXXII.F.21. © Ashmolean Museum, University of Oxford.

The reflecting mirror of fame is seen in a mid-nineteenth-century engraving of Sir Walter Scott at the monuments to Dante and Michelangelo in the Florentine church of Santa Croce (fig. 24). The memorial to Dante here had been erected, in the absence of the poet's remains, by Florentine nationalists in time for the 500th anniversary of his death in 1821. Scott, whose immensely popular novels spoke to the Romantic love of history as a repository of heroic values and freedom, and who inspired many early-nineteenth-century European painters, is here remembered (after his own death) paying tribute to the two figures who stood as epitomes of visionary imagination respectively in poetry and visual art. His companion reads aloud from a guide-book, or perhaps from the *Comedy*.

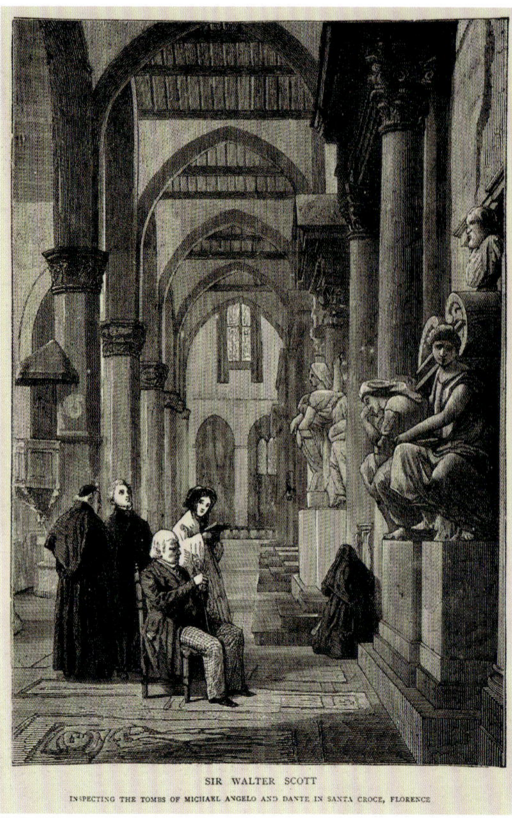

Fig. 24 *Sir Walter Scott inspecting the tombs of Michael Angelo and Dante in Santa Croce, Florence.* Engraving, English, mid-19th century. Private Collection.

The invention of cinema would permanently alter the construction and mediation of fame. At first, however, the new medium struggled to gain respectability. The early shows were short, vulgar and superficial. The decision taken by Milano Films in 1911 to make an epic version of *Inferno* was intended to present the new medium as a serious art form: an aura of cultural respectability was to be derived from the reflected glory of the *Comedy*. This high-budget venture was also an affirmation, in the fiftieth anniversary of the foundation of the Italian state, and in the face of status anxieties about over-identification with past glories, of Italy's unique national capacity to bring together classical and Renaissance culture and modern technology. The film was an international success, grossing $2 million in the United States alone, and it would greatly influence later directors, including Roberto Rossellini and Federico Fellini (fig. 25).

A decade later, in September 1921, Charlie Chaplin came to London to promote his new film. *The Kid* was one of the first to combine comedy and drama, a controversial mixture of genres that was also characteristic of the *Comedy*. The poor boy from south London returned from the United States as a celebrity. In his autobiography Chaplin wrote:

> I chose the Ritz Hotel because it had just been built when I was a boy and, passing its entrance, I had caught a glimpse of the gilt and splendour inside, and ever since I had had a curiosity to know how the rest of it looked. An enormous crowd was waiting outside the hotel and I made a little speech. When at last I was settled in

> the rooms my impatience to get out alone was excruciating. But the milling crowds were outside, shouting their greetings, and I was obliged to go on the balcony several times and, like royalty, acknowledge their cheers.[5]

In a characteristic gesture which became famous, Chaplin took a large bunch of carnations from his room and scattered the flowers to the crowd below.

In the following days the London press reported extensively on the celebrations in Italy to mark the 600th anniversary of the death of Dante on 14 September. On that date *The Times* issued a free, sixteen-page 'Dante' supplement, which celebrated Dante for a readership assumed to have at least some familiarity with the *Comedy*: 'Six hundred years have passed, and today the appeal of the great poem is wider and stronger than in any former age.' A contemporary cartoon in *Punch* captured the encounter, in London, of these two figures of universal fame (fig. 26). Their mirrored exchange in the caption plays ironically on different kinds of celebrity jostling for

Fig. 25 Dante and Virgil in the Circle of the Thieves (*Inferno* XXV). Still from L'INFERNO, 1911, directed by Francesco Bertolini, Adolfo Padovan, Giuseppe De Liguoro; restored by Fondazione Cineteca di Bologna; © Fondazione Cineteca di Bologna.

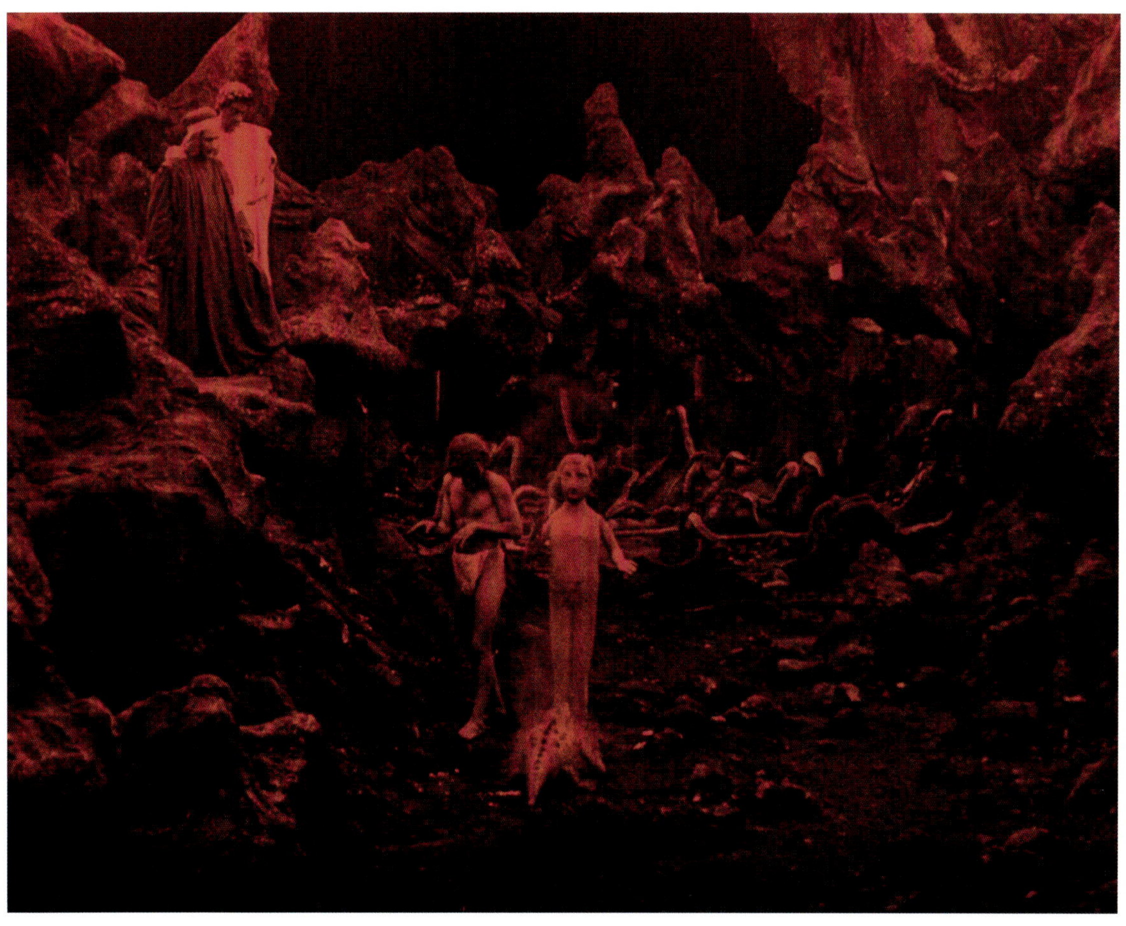

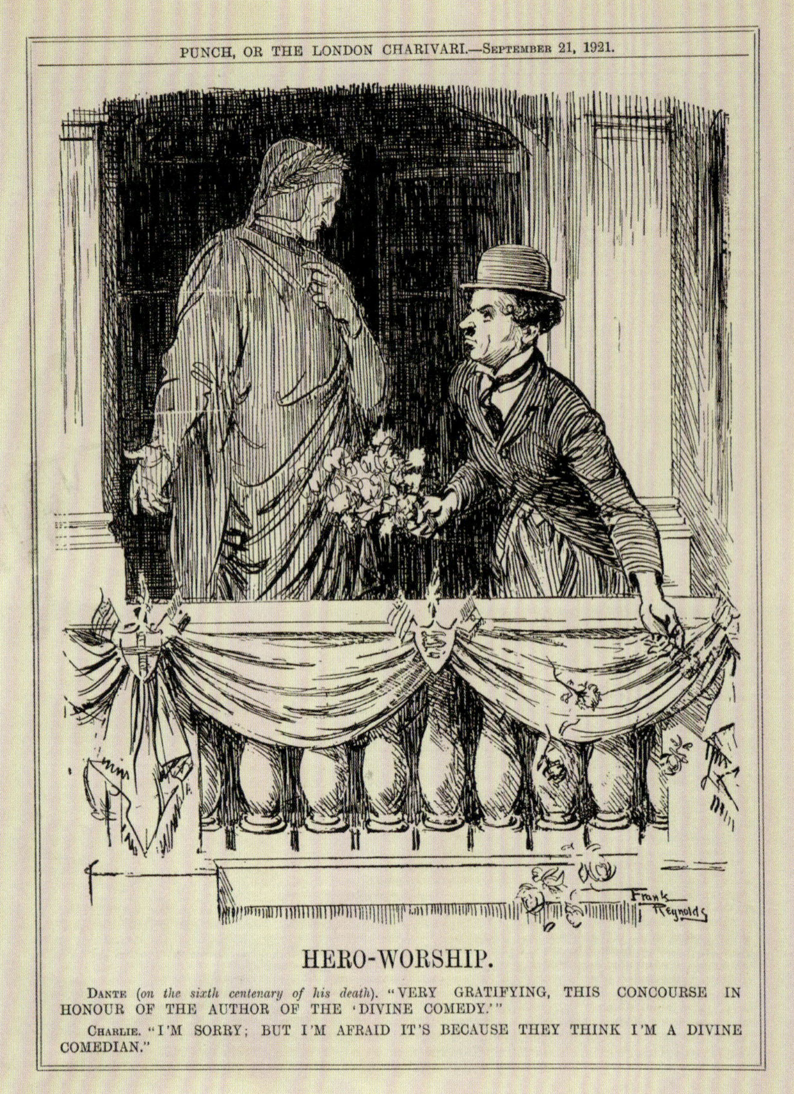

Fig. 26 'Hero-Worship': Dante and Charlie Chaplin respond to the crowd. *Punch, or The London Charivari*, 21 September 1921. Private Collection.

the attention of the same audience. 'Dante (on the sixth centenary of his death): "Very gratifying, this concourse in honour of the author of the *Divine Comedy*." Charlie: "I'm sorry, but I'm afraid it's because they think I'm a Divine Comedian."'

By the late 1940s the star of *Casablanca*, *For Whom the Bell Tolls* and *Gaslight* was so famous that *The Associated Press* named her 'Woman of the Year in America'. Hollywood felt itself responsible for that fame, which partly explains the criticism which attended Ingrid Bergman's move to Italy and marriage to Roberto Rossellini, the maker of very different, neorealist films. Away from the idealising artifice of Hollywood, she made films with Rossellini including *Stromboli*, *Viaggio in Italia* (*Journey to Italy*) and *La Paura*

(*Fear*) which were commercial failures at the time, but which are now recognised as key foundation-stones of modern cinema. At the end of her Italian period, Bergman chose to be photographed face to face with Dante: another famous realist, in addition to being the epitome of the universal status of European culture (fig. 27; cover image). The photographer, Mario Carrieri, who would later become a distinguished photographer of sculpture, was himself closely associated with the neorealist tendency of the 1950s in Italy. The affinity between actor, poet and photographer makes this a perfect example of the construction of fame in the image of Dante.

Today we live in an age of spectacle, in which an infinity of images are consumed by audiences evidently satisfied with superficial celebrity; the demand for substantive content to the image is in decline. Perhaps we exaggerate the novelty of our situation: the ancients, as we have seen, already reflected on the delicate relationship between appearance and reality. There is at least, however, a difference of degree: the global media of postmodernity threaten to reduce culture to a series of two-dimensional icons, mutually interchangeable and infinitely reproduced. Reflecting on a world in which culture is celebrity – nothing more – in 2006 the Taiwanese artists

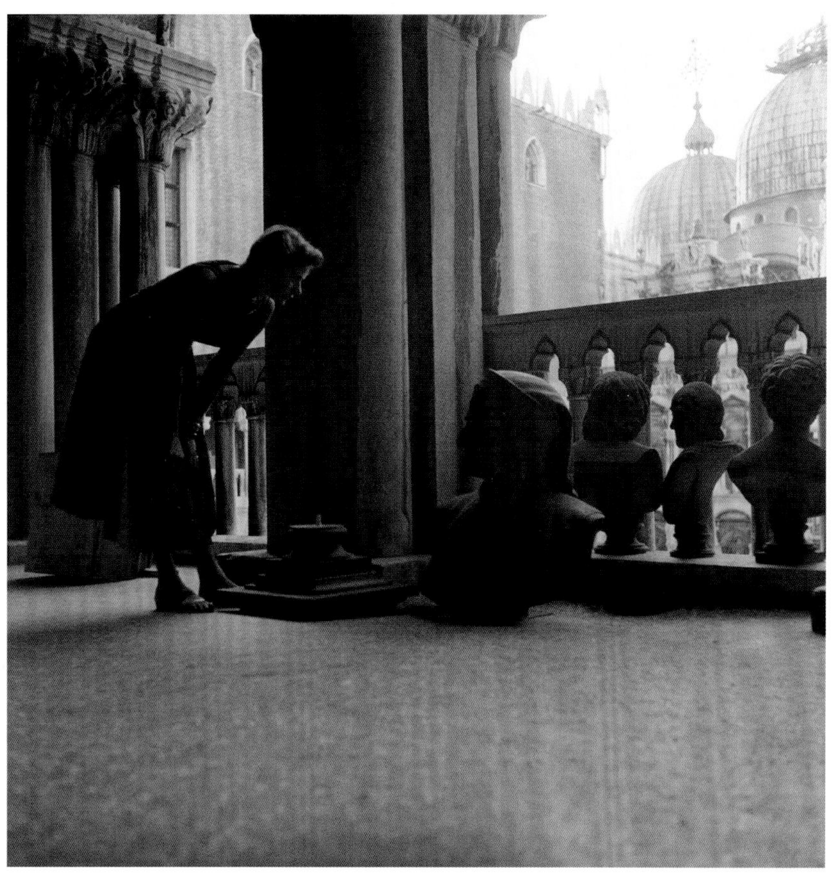

Fig. 27 Ingrid Bergman observing a bust of Dante under a portico in Venice, 1955. Photograph by Mario Carrieri via Getty Images.

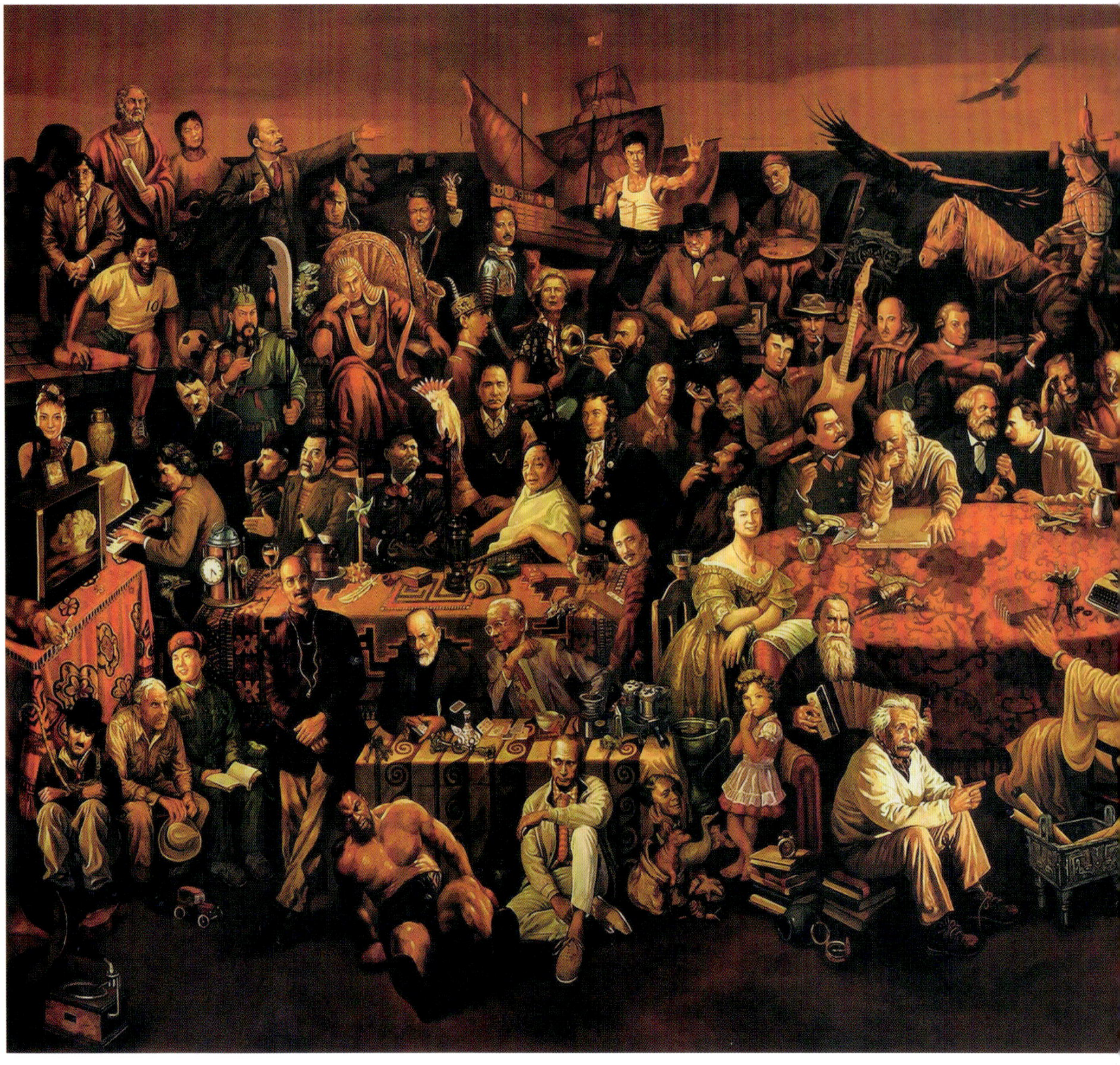

Fig. 28 Dai Dudu, Li Tiezi and Zhang An, *Discussing the Divine Comedy with Dante*, 2006. © The artists.

Dai Dudu, Li Tiezi and Zhang An painted a vast canvas (6 × 2.6 metres) called *Discussing the Divine Comedy with Dante* (fig. 28). Mediated by the Internet, this work became a digital sensation. Just over a hundred famous characters are depicted in conversation about the work of the famous poet, who is seen standing on a terrace to the right of the picture. Close to Dante, rubbing shoulders with fame, the artists depicted themselves. The image captures an idea of the *Comedy* itself as celebrity. The composition draws inspiration (and claims status by association) from Raphael's frescoes in the papal apartments of the Vatican, *The School of Athens* and the *Disputa*, which also parade celebrities of art and science – including Dante (see

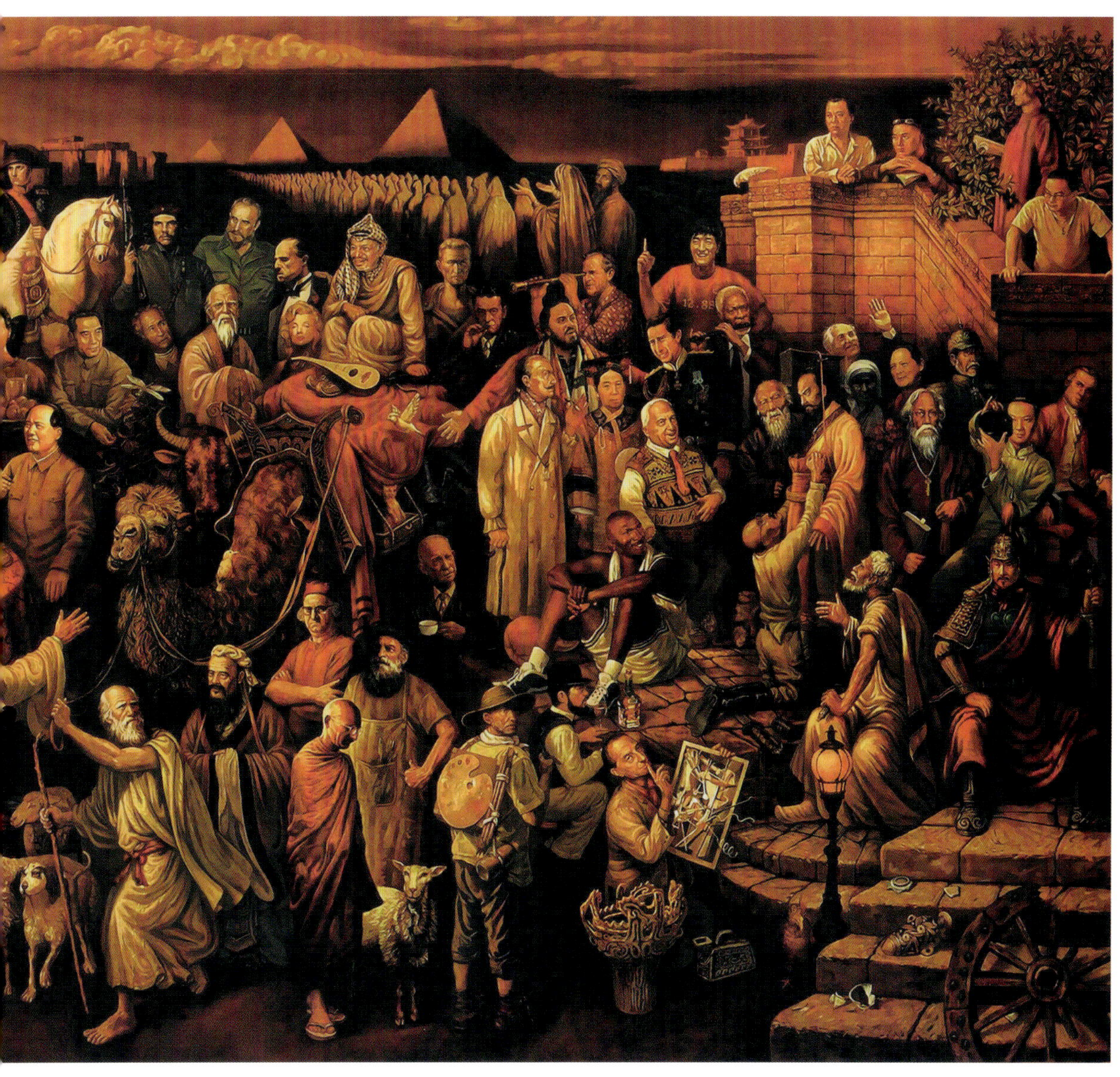

fig. 10). *Discussing the Divine Comedy with Dante* is an apotheosis of one of the world's most famous symbols of culture, which is seen to be infinitely reflected in this galaxy of other luminaries. Among those represented are Socrates, Confucius, Lenin, Shakespeare, Mozart, Ho Chi Minh, Mother Teresa, Ghandi, Audrey Hepburn, Beethoven, Picasso, Charlie Chaplin, Marilyn Monroe and Elvis Presley. Beyond the parlour game of identifying the portraits, the picture ironises the way in which modern global culture has become obsessed with celebrity, to the extent that iconic portrait images such as these are of greater interest to most of us than the content of the *Divine Comedy* itself. Superficial familiarity is all.

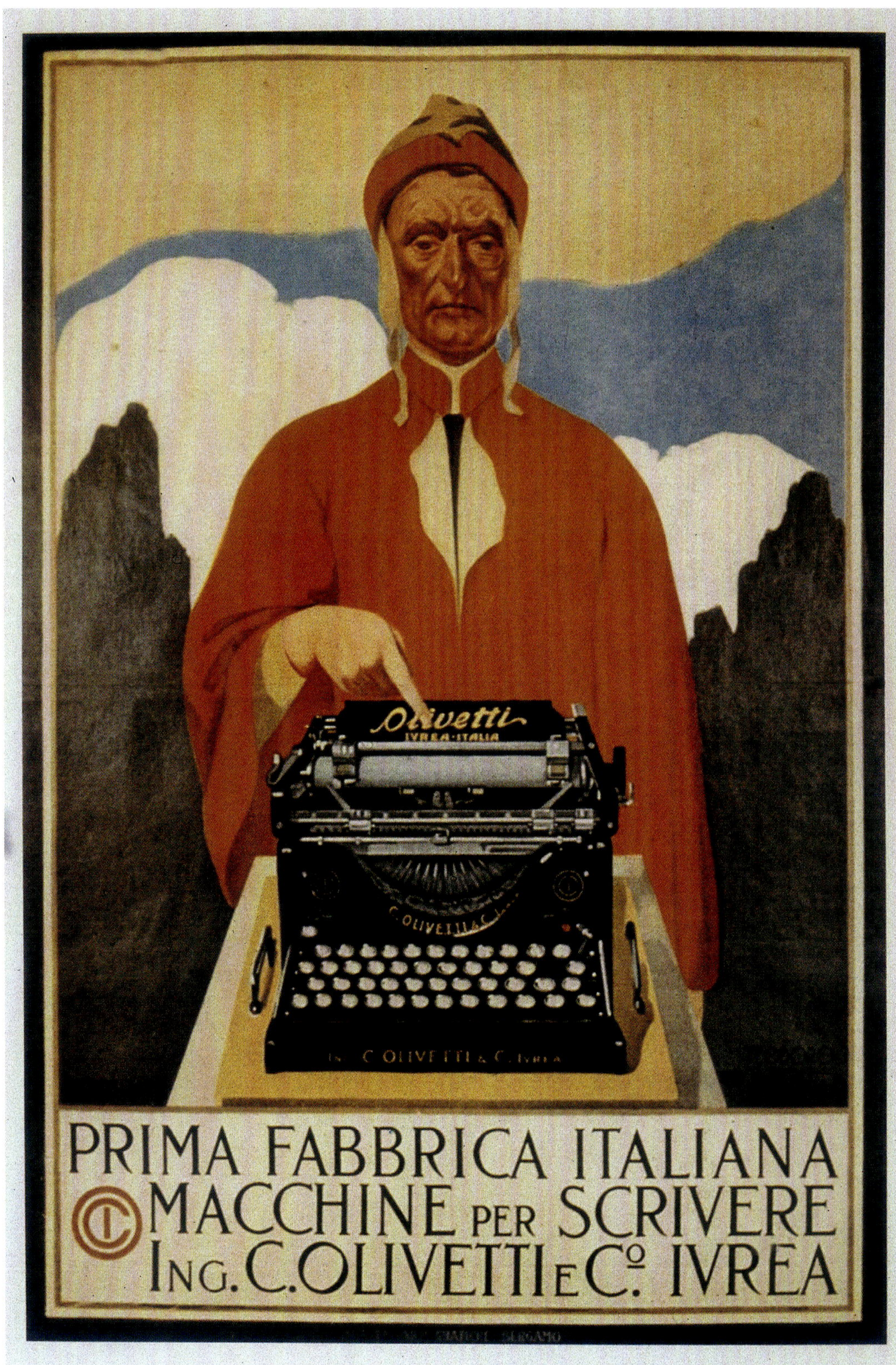
Olivetti
IVREA·ITALIA
PRIMA FABBRICA ITALIANA
MACCHINE PER SCRIVERE
ING. C. OLIVETTI E C.º IVREA

Fig. 29 Publicity poster for Olivetti typewriter, 1911. Illustration by Teodoro Wolf Ferrari (1878–1945). Fondazione Alinari per la Fotografia – Regione Toscana. Alinari Archives, Florence.

Fig. 30 Dante prepares to leave Florence on a diplomatic mission to the pope in Rome. Italian advertisement for the Liebig Extract of Meat Company, c.1920. Bodleian Libraries, University of Oxford, John Johnson Collection, Food 10 (4e).

In a capitalist market, fame has its price, and can be instrumentalised in the service of the most diverse interests. The nineteenth-century boom of enthusiasm for Dante coincided with the birth of the age of mass advertising. Especially, but not only, in Italy, Dante has been recruited to boost the sales of innumerable products, from package tours to tile filler ('Arcansas re-writes the *Paradise* of do-it-yourself', with an image of Dante holding a filler gun under his arm) to cars (an Italian TV advertisement of 2008 insisted, mis-quoting a famous speech made by Ulysses in *Inferno* XXVI: 'You were not born to live as brutes, but to buy a Fiat').

Emblematic of the recruitment of the author of the *Comedy* to sell the products of the modern economy is a poster of 1911 advertising the original Olivetti typewriter (fig. 29). The company had very recently been founded near Turin, and it was at the World Fair held in that city in 1911 that the first machine, the M1, was launched. The company's founder, Camillo Olivetti, was almost certainly responsible for summoning Dante to the cause. The image by Wolf Ferrari is a collage of a modern photograph of the typewriter with a more stylised treatment of the figure of Dante and of the background, which recalls late-medieval Italian painting. That combination of cultural tradition with technical modernity was a deliberate bid to position Olivetti at the heart of the new state of Italy at the beginning of the twentieth century.

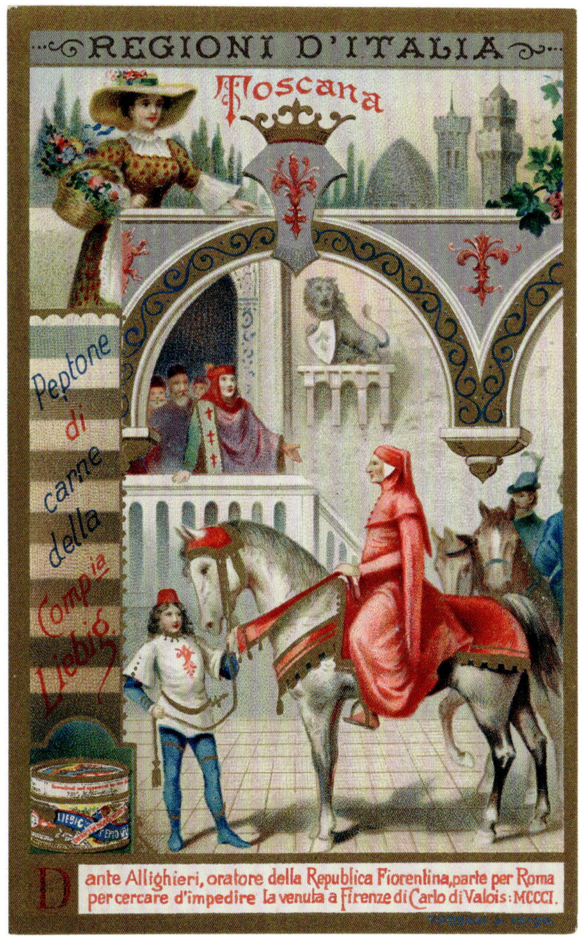

In the same period, the London-based Liebig Company sold tins of meat extract, 'Oxo' stock cubes and corned beef prepared at its meat packaging centre of Fray Bentos in Uruguay. In promotional images issued with the product in Italy, scenes from the life of Dante were used to lend high cultural and patriotic connotations not, perhaps, naturally associated with extract of meat (fig. 30). In one scene Dante is shown about to depart on a diplomatic mission to the pope in Rome, which was shortly followed by the papally supported *coup* which led to Dante's exile from Florence. The lofty subject and historicising costumes and setting are subtly combined with the attractive modern Tuscan woman who admires

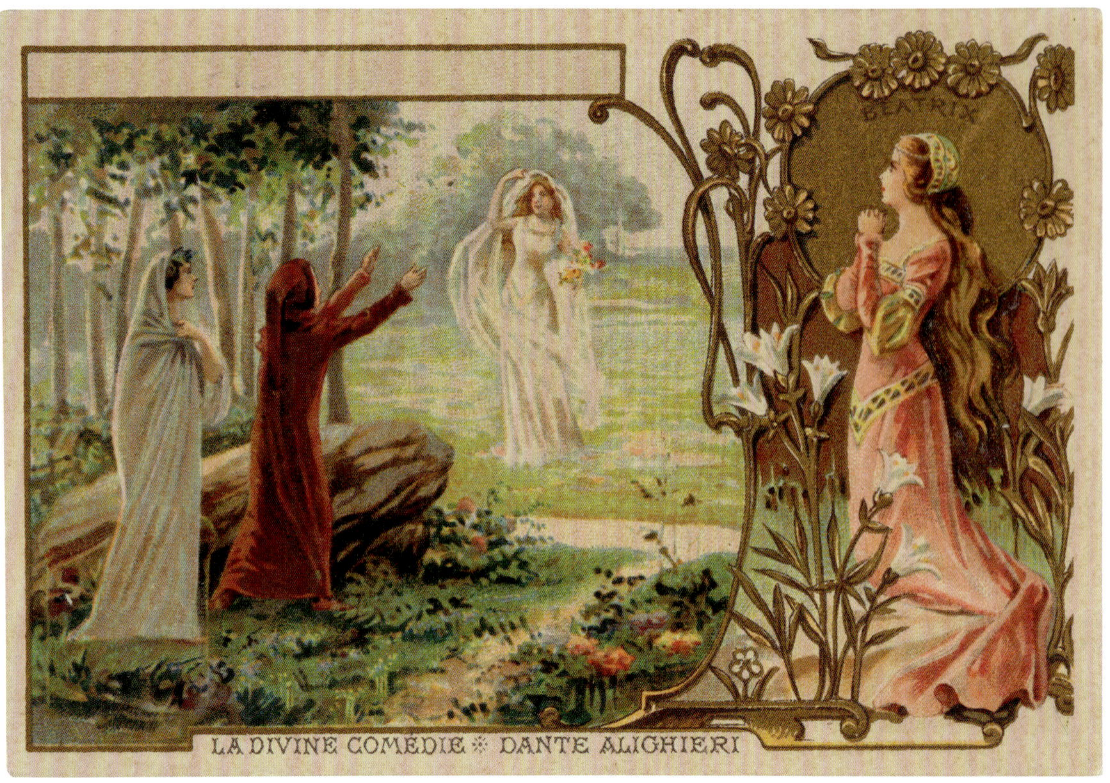

Fig. 31 Advertisement for 'Chicorée Extra « A la Belle Jardinière »'. Chromolithograph on card. *c.*1910. Private Collection.

both Dante and Liebig's meat extract. In a similar vein, a company in Lille making chicory, which was essentially marketed as a substitute for coffee, could evidently count on its lower-middle-class market to be familiar with the *Comedy* to the extent of recognising the scene in the Earthly Paradise in which Dante turns from Virgil to meet the graceful Matelda, while Beatrice looks on (*Paradiso* XXVIII) (fig. 31).

When, again at the turn of the twentieth century, the Genoese firm of Costa began to export olive oil to the Americas and Australia, they needed a name which would identify their product as unmistakeably 'Italian'. The branding of 'Olio Dante' which followed in 1903 has proved so successful that other producers in Spain and Italy have more recently created their own 'Beatrice' olive oils (figs 32–34). In due course marketing expanded into the new medium of television. Around 1960 the magazine advertisement 'Olio Dante is my secret' ran concurrently with a TV 'spot' featuring the popular actor Peppino De Filippo as 'Peppino cuoco sopraffino' (Peppino the most refined cook): his portrait appeared in the lower corner of the image. Peppino's jingle ran: 'Se il buon vino fa sempre buon sangue / che miracoli fa l'olio Dante' ('If good wine makes good blood, / What miracles Olio Dante works').

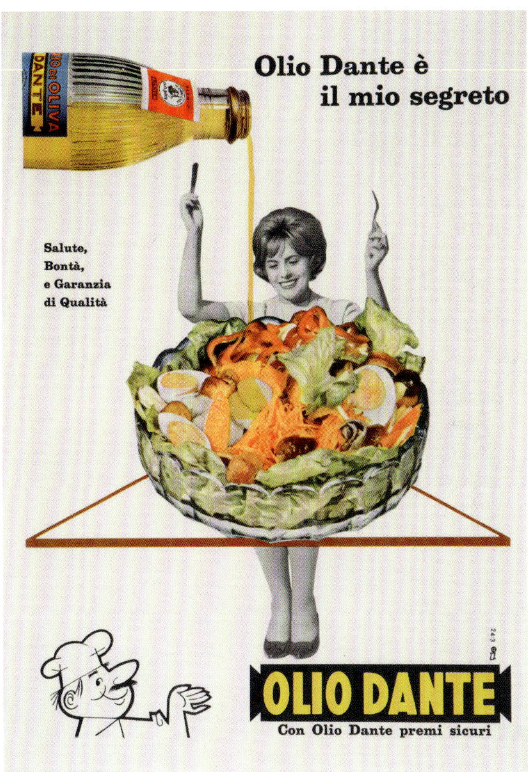

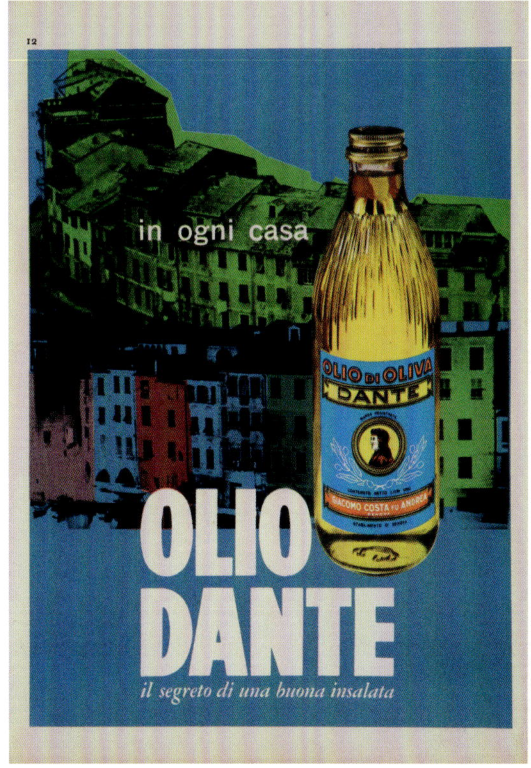

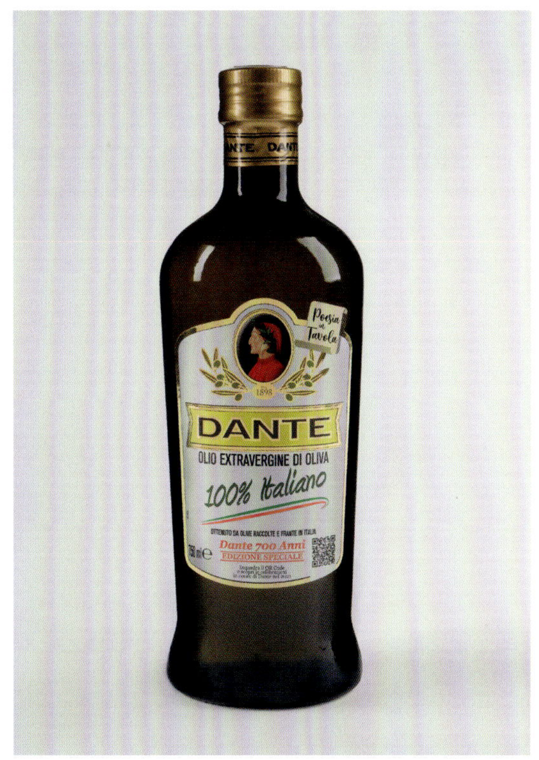

Top left:
Fig. 32 'Olio Dante è il mio segreto.' Advertisement, *c.*1960. Olio Dante, with permission.

Top right:
Fig. 33 Advertisement for Olio Dante *c.*1960. Olio Dante, with permission.

Bottom right:
Fig. 34 Olio Dante olive oil. Private Collection.

The reason why Dante enjoys instant recognition in commercial advertising lies in the nature of the *Comedy* itself. The work was, from the start, a paradox: a cultural statement of the highest order, expressed in the language of the street. Some of Dante's more scholarly contemporaries raised an eyebrow at the choice, not of Latin, but of vulgar Tuscan – intermingled, indeed, with a cacophony of other languages and dialects of the Italian peninsula – as the language of his visionary poem. The vernacular was, in the words of a contemporary letter possibly written by Dante himself, deliberately selected as the language 'in which even women converse': even, that is, people without formal education or literacy. The 800 or so manuscripts of the *Comedy* which survive from the fourteenth and fifteenth centuries (no doubt only a fraction of the original total) testify to the huge publishing success of the work even prior to the invention of the printing press. But perhaps even more importantly the poem circulated orally, becoming part of a rich tradition, which until recently played an enormous role in embedding Dante and his work in popular culture. Stories told in Tuscany at the end of the fourteenth century by Francesco Sacchetti describe a peasant and a blacksmith overheard by the poet himself singing, at their work, passages of the *Comedy*. In the tales, Dante is presented as annoyed by the mangling of his rhythms by these working-class performers – but neither surprised at nor critical of their familiarity with the poem. That popular currency of the poem, at least in Italy, has never died out: today in the Tuscan village of Panzano in Chianti a butcher, Dario Cecchini, entertains his customers with his knowledge, by heart, of the entire poem. Apart from such informal recitation, public renditions of the *Comedy* have continued from the 1370s, when regular readings and commentaries began for mixed audiences in the cathedral in Florence, to the early-twenty-first-century performances to vast audiences, staged and experienced much like pop concerts, by the comedian Roberto Benigni.

The choice of language, although crucial, is only part of the key to the accessibility of the *Comedy* and to the universality of its fame. Equally significant is the inclusiveness of Dante's human perspective. The tolerance of the *Comedy* – its openness to diverse readers – is startling. Dante does not judge social groups; rather, he questions the motivation of individuals, whoever they may be. His Christian perspective constrains what can be said about Muslims, as about pagans who lived before Christ. Yet although on the one hand both Mohammed and his son-in-law Ali are placed by Dante (significantly alongside Christians, including Bertran de Born (see fig. 5), who were equally culpable) in the Hell of those who caused division where there should be unity, on the other hand he put in Limbo, alongside the virtuous pagans, the Muslim ruler Saladin (1138–93) and the Muslim philosophers

Avicenna (980–1037) and Averroes (1126–98). Even more strikingly, in the heavenly circle of the just Dante asks rhetorically why someone cannot be saved, merely because they are born somewhere beyond the bounds of Christianity – on the banks of the Indus, for example. 'Where is the justice in his condemnation? / Is it his fault, if he does not have faith?' (*Paradiso* XIX 76–7). The answer which is offered – that divine justice is invisible to human sight – patently side-steps the question, which is returned to a few lines later when the reader is told that there are 'Ethiopians' – black, non-Christian inhabitants of Africa – alive today who, at the last judgement, will be closer to God than hypocritical Christians who presently proclaim Christ's name: 'see how many shout aloud: "Christ! Christ!" / Who on the Day of Judgement will be farther / From Him than those who never heard of Christ' (*Paradiso* XIX 106–8). Dante does not explicitly state that such Ethiopians 'who never heard of Christ' will be saved for eternity; but this is a legitimate reading of the lines.

From the opening line of the story, 'Nel mezzo del cammin di *nostra* vita' ('Half-way along *our* journey to life's end'), every reader finds themself implicated in the experiences of the pilgrim who goes by the name of Dante. The themes of the poem, which concern the existential destruction wrought by human selfishness and the possibility of redemption through generous engagement with others, are universal; yet they are rooted in the specific experiences of the infinitely various characters encountered on the journey. The radical inclusiveness of Dante's vision of humanity – deliberately echoed much later by Balzac, when he chose to call his novelistic panorama of nineteenth-century French society *La Comédie humaine* (*The Human Comedy*) – offers infinite possibilities for the reader or listener to enter into identification with the personalities who are so vividly conjured into being. Those of us who join the pilgrim for the unpredictable and altogether extraordinary journey which unfolds from that opening line must be willing to give up life as we know it; but no-one is excluded from the experience.

Just as the many voices of the *Comedy* communicate in different registers, so we find responses to Dante taking diverse forms which cross conventional distinctions between 'high' and 'low' culture. The surge of Dante readership in the nineteenth century familiarised an ever-wider public with the various episodes of the poem, so that these became familiar touchstones of daily life. When, in the Paris Salon of 1822, Delacroix displayed *The Barque of Dante*, he knew that his choice of subject – Dante and Virgil being ferried by Phlegyas across the River Styx (*Inferno* VIII) – would appeal to judges and public alike. As though to underline the extent to which Dante was in the air, Delacroix had the *Comedy* read aloud to him while he worked at his easel, and attended a fancy-dress ball dressed as the poet. His painting was immediately acquired for the nation and displayed in the

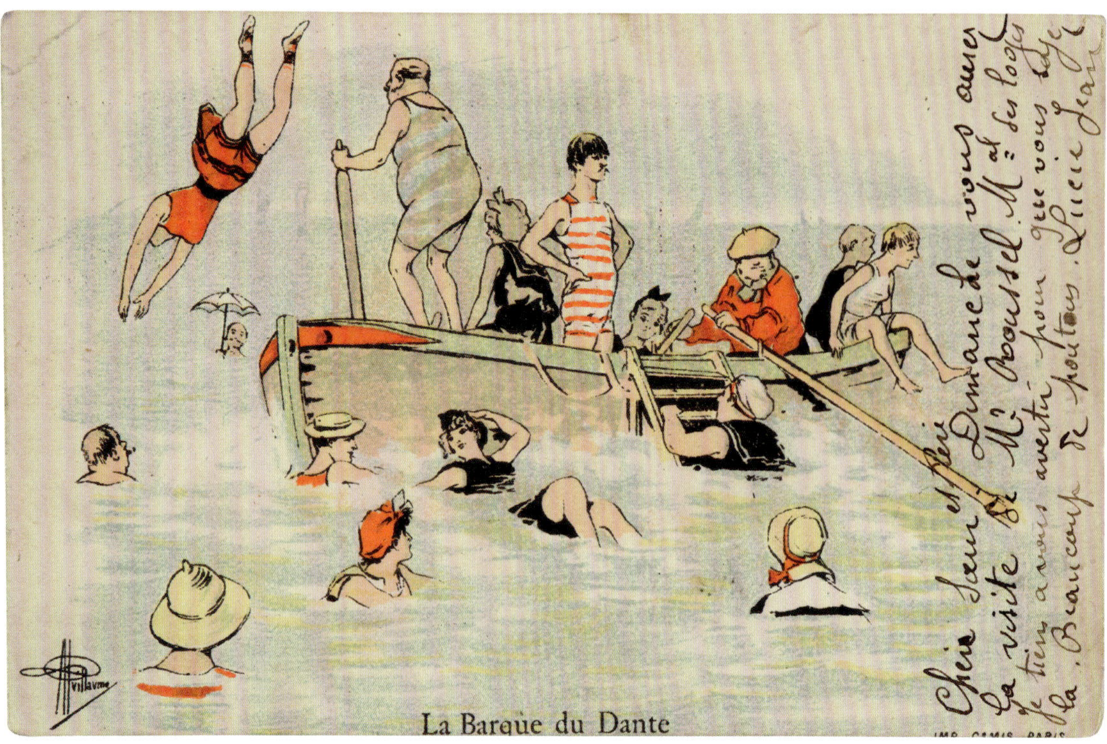

Fig. 35 'La Barque du Dante'. Postcard, *c.*1900. Private Collection.

Louvre. Eighty or so years later this high-status salon painting found its commonplace avatar in a postcard – that most popular and universal of all media in the decades around 1900 – which referenced both Delacroix and Dante (fig. 35).

Like Delacroix, Gustave Doré too sought, by associating himself with Dante, to elevate his cultural standing and fame. Doré had found his ambitions as an artist frustrated by his reputation as a mere illustrator, and he hoped through engagement with Dante to promote both his medium of engraving and himself. The first publication of Doré's engravings of the *Comedy* alongside the poem in the 1860s was a deliberate attempt by artist and publisher to enhance the text with memorable images, and thereby to secure for the illustrated book the status of high art (see figs 5, 42). These images have sometimes been deprecated as the work – after all – of a mere illustrator; but this is unjust to the attention which Doré gave to the selection of details in the poem for representation, and to his ability to create an atmosphere suited to the episode in hand. His very success – these engravings have been endlessly reproduced in popular editions of the poem down to today – has left a question over his standing as a fine artist. Yet his series of images, in acquiring a certain celebrity for their author, have also contributed significantly to the fame of Dante himself. For many, Doré has been the first point of contact with the *Comedy*.

Dramatic representations of individual scenes from the *Comedy*, which had begun much earlier, proliferated from the nineteenth century, further increasing the currency of Beatrice, Francesca of Rimini, and other characters in the poem. They include La Pia, a soul encountered on the lower slopes of the mountain of Purgatory about whom little is known except that she was Sienese and that she was murdered by her husband. Her gentle character is suggested by the lines Dante gives her:

> Please remember me, who am La Pia.
> Siena made me, in Maremma I was undone.
> He knows how, the one who, to marry me,
> first gave the ring that held his stone. (*Purgatorio* v 130–36)

During the nineteenth century La Pia inspired numerous poems, plays and romantic novels. An especially ambitious and high-profile play, Gabriele d'Annunzio's vast *Francesca da Rimini* of 1901, would prompt the making of an early silent film. In turn, some fifty cinematic versions of the *Comedy* have followed across the twentieth century, and if quality has often fallen short of ambition, they remain testimony to the perceived popular appeal of Dante's story. Beyond the vernacular popularity which cinema shares with the *Comedy*, one feature in particular lends the medium an affinity with the poem. As we watch the Milano Films *Inferno* of 1911, the shades of the dead which move across the screen, indexically linked as they are to the living actors, perform to near-perfection the role given to them in Dante's poem: they repeat in death, to eternity, what they were in life (see fig. 25). Other films, rather than attempting to present the narrative in Dante's terms, have contextualised the *Comedy* in modern situations. One of the best, *Dante's Inferno* of 1935, produced by Harry Lachman and starring Spencer Tracy, tells a Dantesque moral tale through the fortunes of a fairground attraction called 'Dante's Inferno'. The film includes a powerful evocation of Hell itself, for which the director borrowed passages from the 1911 version by Milano Films: the mediation of the *Comedy* becomes ever more layered as it penetrates the larger culture.

Dante's entry into the world of cartoons was marked by a similar economy of mutual benefit. *Mickey Mouse in Hell* was the first in the series of Mickey's adventures to be commissioned from Italian designers (Guido Martina and Angelo Bioletto), and was published in five numbers in 1949–50. Cartoons had hitherto been seen, especially in Italy, as children's fare only: Disney's embrace of Dante (echoing the *Comedy*'s cinematic début in the early 1900s) marked a watershed for the development of the medium as a more serious art form. On the other hand, it amplified the fame of Dante in yet wider cultural circles. In one of the opening frames, Mickey, lost in the dark wood (including a knowing visual quotation of a tree from the equivalent scene by Doré), is assailed by wild beasts (fig. 36). Fleeing,

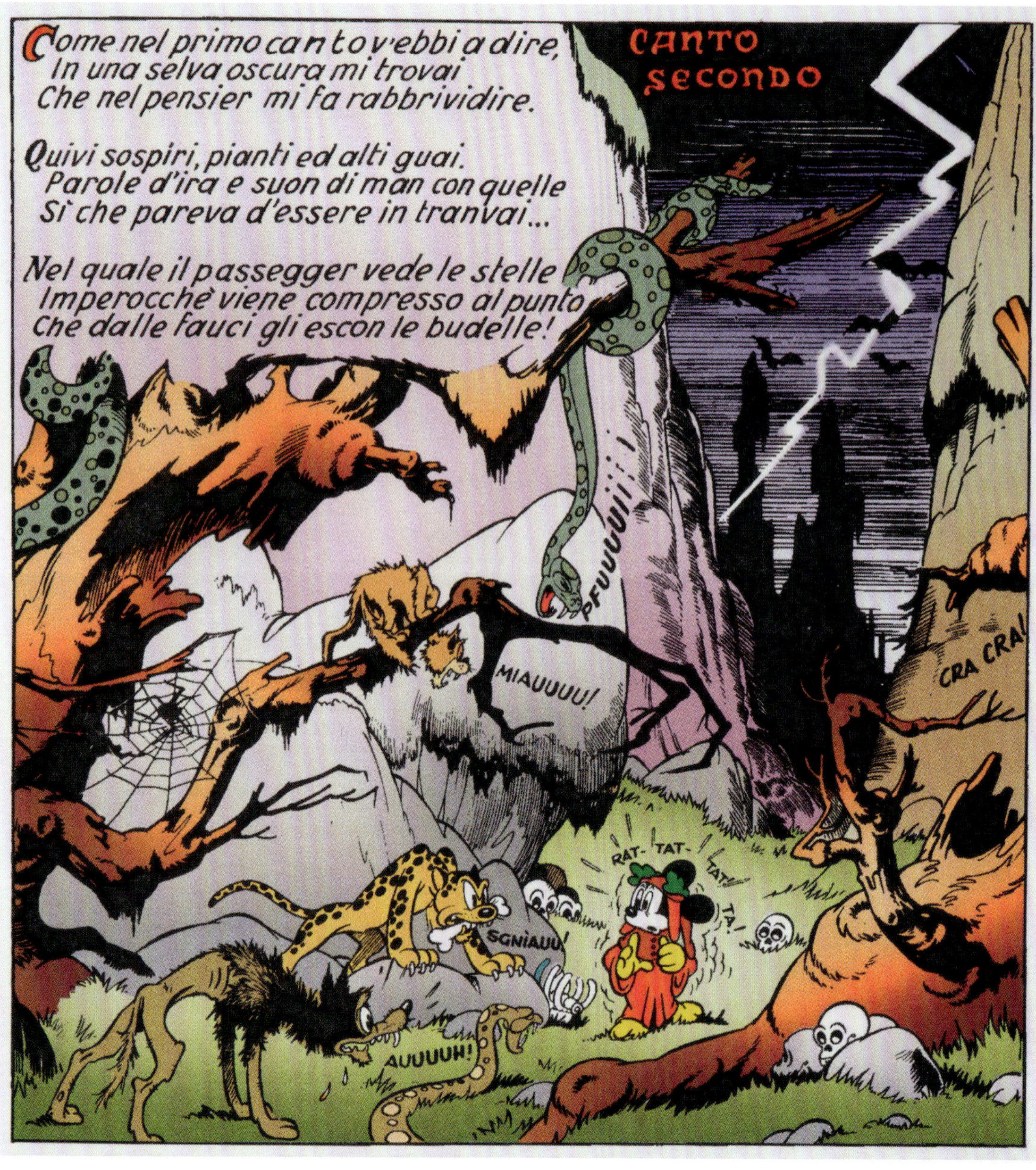

Fig. 36 Topolino nell'Inferno (Mickey Mouse in Hell). Disney Corporation, 1949. © Disney Corporation.

he meets Pluto (Pippo in Italian), who will be his 'Virgil'. The accompanying rhymes wittily re-write the poem in Dantesque tercets, with constant quotations and echoes of the original. At the same time, the narrative is adapted to its post-war Italian context, and where Dante had condemned the Florence of his own day, the cartoon version inveighs against football corruption, government malpractice and overcrowded trams.

From the next generation, the cartoonist Marcello Toninelli (b. 1950) worked on his version of the *Comedy* for more than four decades (fig. 37).

The theme of worldly fame in the age of mass media is central to Toninelli's creative response to the poem. Beatrice appears as an attractive presenter called Bea Trix, and as artistic director of programmes in Paradise is preoccupied with the management of her staff and the popularity index. Thomas Aquinas echoes the media personality Mike Bongiorno with 'The Wheel of Culture', in a parody of a television show called 'The Wheel of Fortune'. 'The Saint Bonaventure Show' satirises the famous 'Maurizio Costanzo Show', in this case with the blessed souls, in the place of models, filing across the stage. Angelina Jolie and Brad Pitt make personal appearances, adding to the impression of the *Comedy* as an extended parody of star culture. For all the playful humour, Toninelli captures the essence of Dante's critique of worldly celebrity. At the end, returning to Italy after his vision, Dante is asked in Toninelli's version whether he will write a poem about it. 'What? And be hated by every schoolchild?' is the answer. 'No – I'll make it a cartoon.'

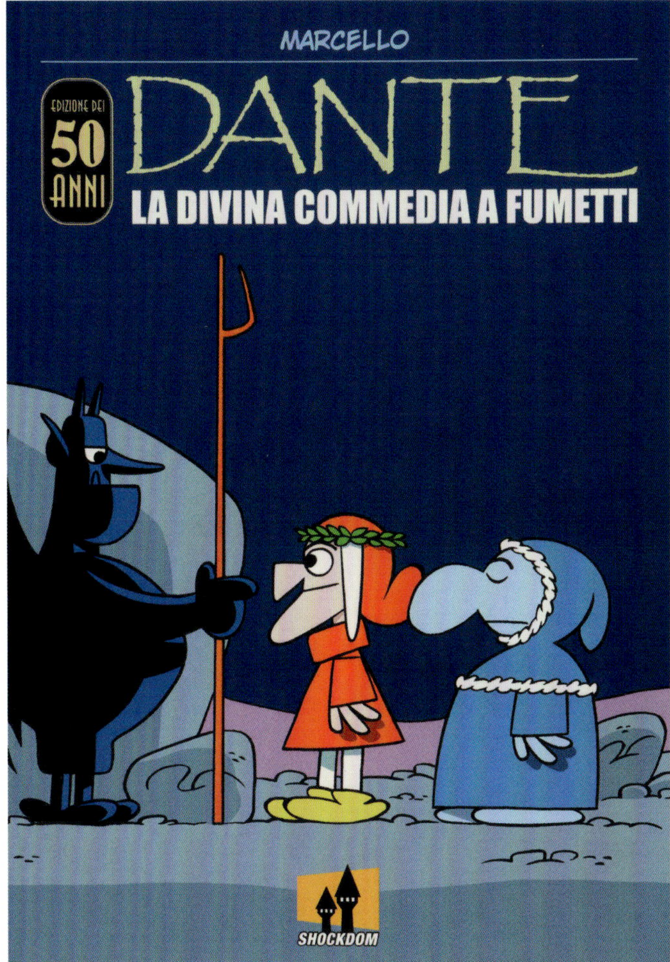

Fig. 37 Marcello, *Dante. La Divina Commedia a fumetti* (Brescia: Shockdom, 2015). By permission of the author and publisher.

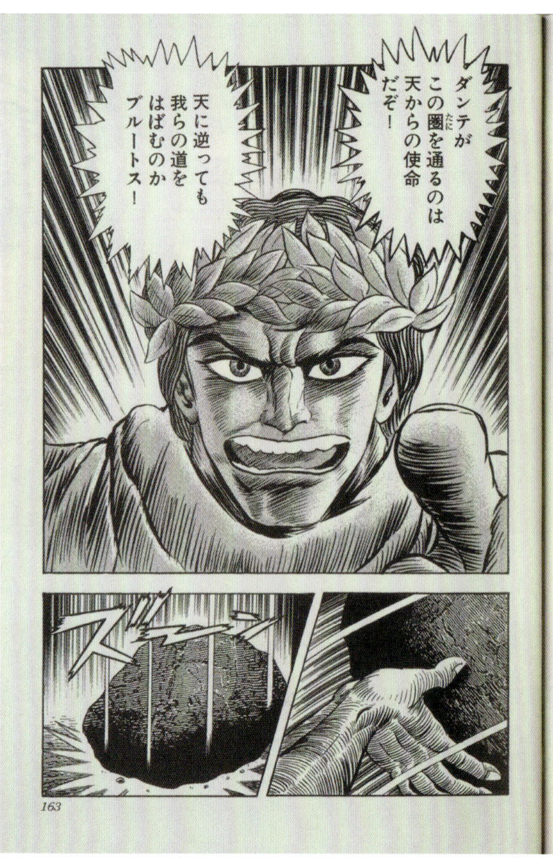

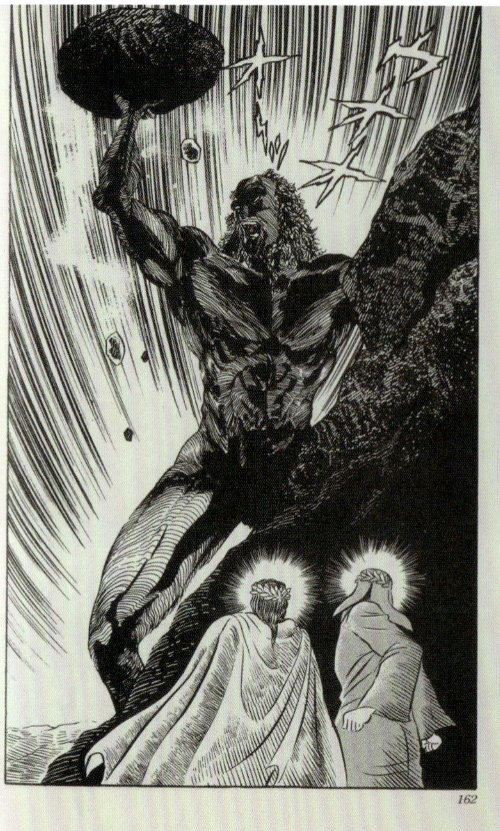

Fig. 38 Nagai Go (b. 1945), *Dante Shinkyoku* (1994). © The artist. Dante and Virgil encounter Pluto, guardian of the circle in Hell of the avaricious and the prodigal (*Inferno* VI).

Each new mediation of the poem is a form of translation, which also reconfigures the image of its author. A paradox of fame which is well illustrated by the case of Dante is that in order to endure, a reputation must adapt, picking up in the process something of the accent of its latest audience. The manga version of the *Comedy* by Go Nagai (b. 1945) is not an attempt to translate Dante's verse for a Japanese audience so much as a creative re-working of the story in the medium of manga. Nagai (whose work was published in 1994) adopted an authorial role, not only selecting which scenes to depict but also including, as occasion demanded, text boxes with supplementary information to help a modern Japanese audience follow the story. He also partially altered Dante's Christian conception of Hell as unchanging, to give instead an idea of continuous flux: a Buddhist vision. Nagai had encountered the *Comedy* (*Shinkyoku* in Japanese) as a child, in a version with the illustrations of Gustave Doré. The visual inspiration from Doré is made explicit by Nagai's inclusion of his own reproductions of the Doré engravings as milestones throughout *Dante Shinkyoku*. Nagai used a laborious technique employing parallel lines to imitate the effect of engraving. At the same time, he drew on the visual language of horror films. Such eclectic borrowings are typical of the manga artist. (fig. 38) The techniques of realism which are particular to his medium correspond well to the poem; the adaptation of the content, on the other hand, represents a significant departure. The result both is, and is not, Dante.

Dante's fierce attack on corruption in urban politics, in speeches given to two Florentines, Ciacco in Hell (*Inferno* vi) and Dante's own ancestor Cacciaguida in Paradise (*Paradiso* xvi), resonates strongly with modern readers. In 2004 Sandow Birk reconfigured both the text of *Inferno* and Doré's engravings in the light of postmodern urban America, a process which also recontextualised the poem. Dante becomes in this case a sneaker- and hoodie-wearing slacker, while Hell, figured as Los Angeles, is populated by fast-food stalls, corporate logos, and police helicopters. Satan himself is trapped not in the frozen lake of Dante's vision but in an infernal traffic jam. The vernacular visual style effectively responds to and updates the social and political invective of Dante's poem. In Hell's circle of the Heretics, the Bank of America has penetrated even the infernal city of Dis, where the Florentine faction-leader or *mafioso* Farinata holds a drink from Starbucks and Virgil's cloak bears an advertisement for a commercial sale (fig. 39, and see fig. 42). The vernacular Californian style of the translation also attempts to modernise the text for a materialist readership of the twenty-first century, with less convincing results. Birk and Sanders subsequently produced their versions of *Purgatorio* (set principally in San Francisco) and *Paradiso* (in New York).

The eclecticism of modern visual responses to the *Comedy* answers to the multiplicity of Dante's own references within the poem to stories and images well-known to his first readers. For his *Inferno* of 1983, the artist Tom Phillips chose to abandon altogether the illustration of the narrative, seeking instead equivalents in modern culture for the famous points of reference upon which Dante could draw in the fourteenth century. The pilgrim Dante's relationship to Virgil, his guide and protector in the descent through Hell, is a filial one, and in a characteristic moment, when the two are pursued by devils,

> My guide wasted no time at all in snatching
> Me – as a mother wakened by the roar
> Of burning, and observing flames approaching. (*Inferno* xxxiii 37–9)

Responding to this passage, Phillips cites Picasso's *Guernica*, drawing upon the currency and the connotations of that famous image even as Dante himself so often evoked examples which fame had rendered familiar to his audience (fig. 40).

Dante's adventures in modern popular culture have certainly extended the resonance of his fame, and the most productive of these encounters have not only ridden the waves of new cultural forms but have added new

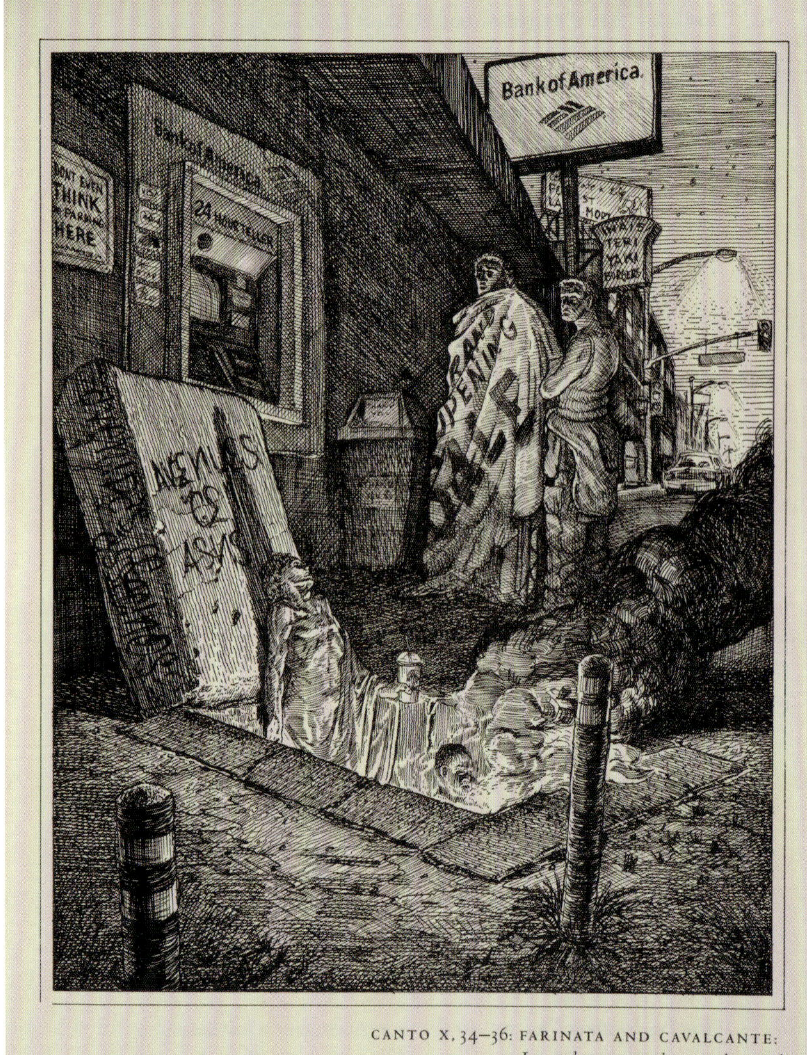

Left:
Fig. 39 *Dante's Inferno* illustrated by Sandow Birk (b. 1962); text adapted by Sandow Birk and Marcus Sanders (San Francisco, CA: Chronicle, 2004). With the artist's permission.

Opposite:
Fig. 40 Tom Phillips (b. 1937), Preparatory print for Canto XXIII of *Dante's Inferno* (published 1983). Bodleian Libraries, University of Oxford. Tom Phillips Collection (Box 140). With the artist's permission.

levels to our appreciation of the *Comedy*. A different judgement might be made of a video game such as 'Dante's Inferno' of 2010, in which the player, acting for Dante, must rescue Beatrice from Hell. Twitter chains which have adopted the Dantesque tercet as a vehicle for political satire, though witty in themselves, simply depend upon the *Comedy* for their form and give nothing back. Sometimes 'Dantesque' is little more than a superficial tag. But – despite the snobbery of the pretentious élite – the *Comedy*'s engagement with a much wider popular culture has been fruitful, because of the roots which were put down in that same soil by Dante himself.

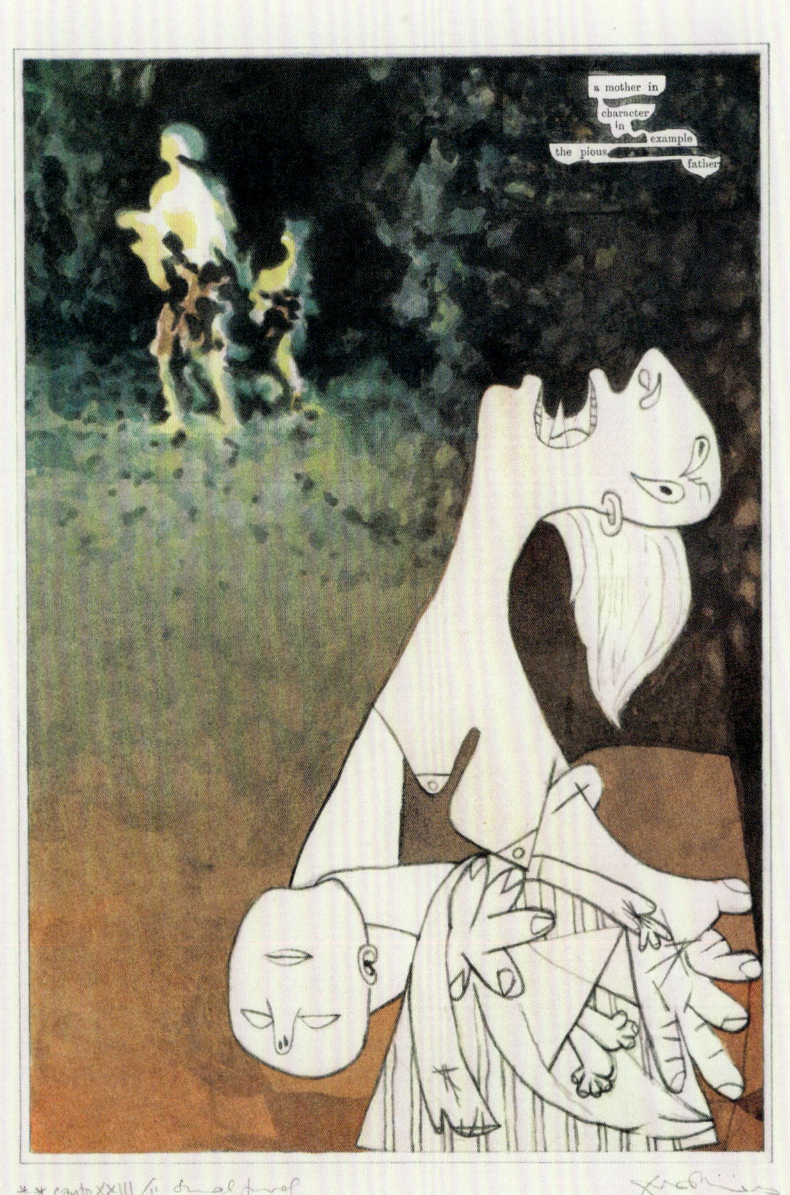
a mother in
character
in
example
the pious
father

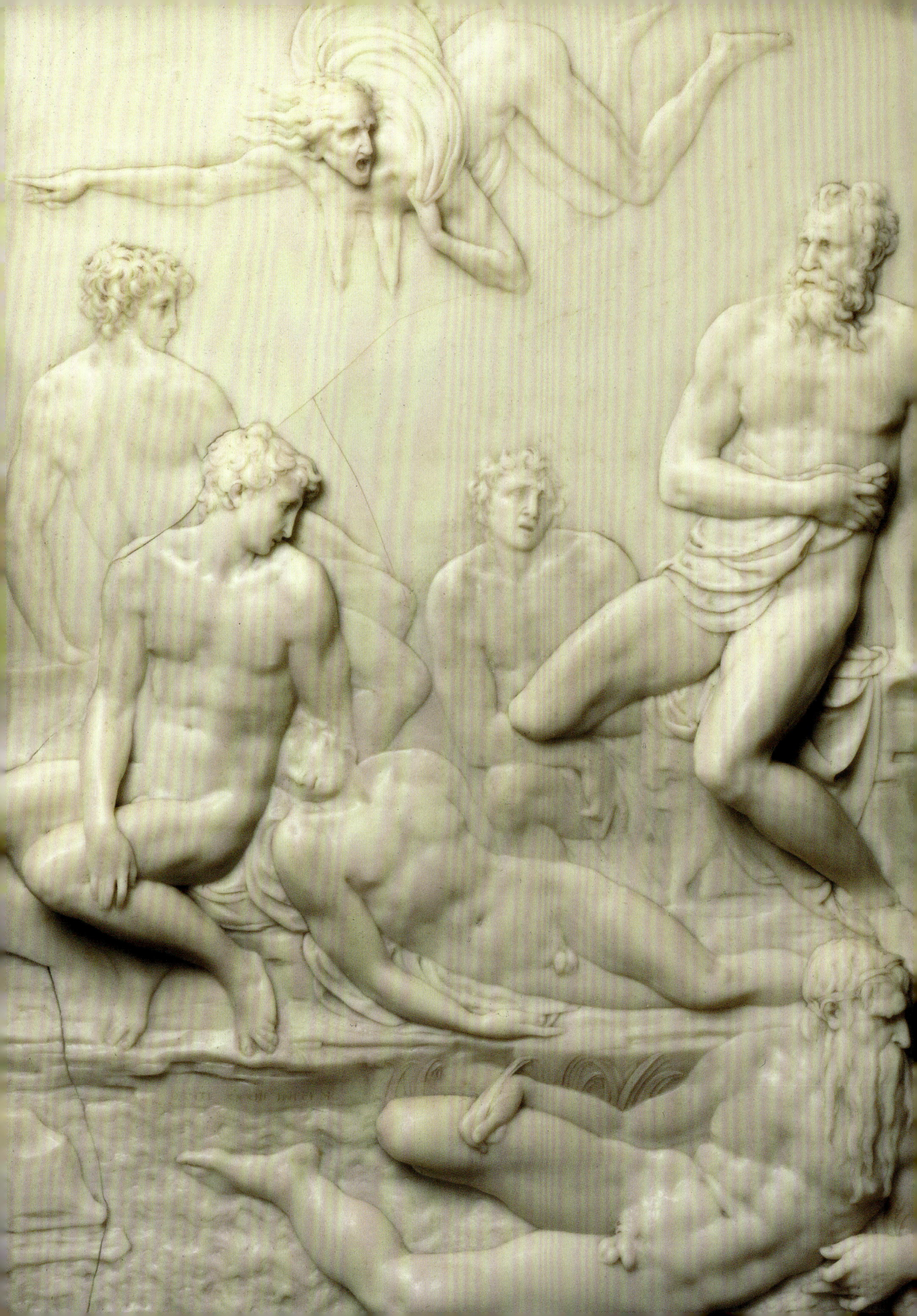

SELECTED HIGHLIGHTS

Fame, we know, is fickle – and selective. In the case of Dante's *Comedy*, this must be so, for no-one could be completely familiar with the poem in its entirety. But the episodic construction of the work deliberately invites the reader to fasten upon particular incidents; to identify with certain characters and emotional moods encountered at different points in the journey. In the history of the *Comedy*'s reception, iconic moments have stood out, generating their own representations and a semi-autonomous status as works of art in their own right. These images of single episodes from the poem have served the taste and concerns of diverse generations of readers, and have at the same time stood as synecdoches for the *Comedy* as a whole. For some, the isolated drama represents the full extent of their familiarity with the *Comedy*. For many others, more extensive readers of Dante, the extracted highlight is seen as distilling some essential element of the poem as a whole.

From the earliest period of its dissemination, the poem was regularly accompanied in manuscripts by illustrations, symptomatic of readers' desire to visualise the narrative and perhaps to add a pictorial commentary to the verse. The first time, however, that we hear of a single incident from the *Comedy* serving as the subject of an independent artwork was the representation in sculptured relief of *Count Ugolino and his Sons in the Tower of Hunger*, created in the late 1540s by Pierino da Vinci (fig. 41). The nephew of Leonardo da Vinci, Pierino was a brilliant follower of Michelangelo who created just a handful of extraordinary works before his death at the age of twenty-five.

The commission came from Luca Martini, a leading amateur scholar of Dante, patron of the composite portrait by Vasari discussed above (see fig. 13), and participant with other leading Tuscans in a project to produce the perfect text of the *Comedy*: their work would result in the major Florentine La Crusca edition of 1595. Martini was governor of Pisa under the Tuscan dukedom of the Medici, and this lent a personal interest to this story of thirteenth-century treachery in Pisa, which had for long been Florence's enemy. But the major reason for the selection of the tragic event, which is narrated by the character of Ugolino himself in Cantos XXXII and XXXIII of *Inferno*, was the pathos of the situation evoked in Dante's verse. A faction-leader who had made himself ruler of Pisa, Count Ugolino was accused, following the city's catastrophic defeat at sea by Genoa in 1284, of treachery. His bitter enemy, Archbishop Ruggiero of Pisa, imprisoned Ugolino together with his sons and grandsons in a tower, where all were left to starve to death. Both characters are encountered in the deepest pit of Dante's Hell, their bodies encased in the ice of Cocytus and ironically forced together in an eternal embrace. In order to relate his horrific story

Fig. 41 Pierino da Vinci (after), (*c.* 1529–53), *Ugolino and his Sons in the Tower of Famine*, 1544–53. Wax, 62 × 45 cm. Ashmolean Museum (WA1897.190). © Ashmolean Museum, University of Oxford.

to the pilgrim Dante, Ugolino pauses momentarily from his grim practice of gnawing on the neck of the archbishop. Although in Dante's perspective both were equally guilty, commentators, moved by the cruel fate of Ugolino's innocent children, identified the scene as one of special pathos. In mid-sixteenth-century Florence, the question was raised whether the great poem could be represented at all in visual art, and if so, whether painting or sculpture might do this better. Benedetto Varchi, who as a prominent member of the Florentine Academy delivered lectures on this subject in the mid-1540s, pronounced that, so far as *Inferno* and *Purgatorio* were concerned, the materiality of sculptural relief would serve better. This was how Ugolino came to be the subject of visual representation in Pierino da Vinci's relief: as a visual epitome of Dante's ability to tell a moving story. Ugolino – whose tragic face is derived from Michelangelo's sculpture of Moses – looks up from the body of his first son to die, while the others await their turn. Below, a river god personifies the Arno, who turns away in horror. The haggard figure of Hunger presides fatally over the scene. Giorgio Vasari wrote at the time that 'no less compassion is stirred by the attitudes shaped in wax by the sculptor in him who beholds them, than is roused in him who listens to the words and accents printed on the living page by the poet'.[6]

Pierino da Vinci's relief endured as a powerful interpretation of Dante's work, especially because it was long attributed to Michelangelo, whose work was indeed a major influence on Pierino. Several copies are known, including two impressions, respectively in wax and terracotta, owned by the Ashmolean Museum. It is likely that both of these were made from moulds taken from the artist's original bronze. (Although improbable, it is not impossible, however, that the former is Pierino's own.) Brought to England around 1700, the bronze was acquired by the 2nd Duke of Devonshire, remaining at Chatsworth until it was sold in 2010. The work inspired an influential painting by Joshua Reynolds, which stands at the head of a flood of nineteenth-century Romantic paintings of Ugolino. In this very different environment, Ugolino continued to be perceived as one of the most famous representatives of the *Comedy*.

The ambivalence which readers feel towards the character of Ugolino is characteristic of many of the personalities created by Dante in his vision of Hell. Each has about them something apparently heroic, whether this be the magnificent arrogance of Farinata, condemned to a burning tomb in the circle of the heretics, who 'Held his chest and held his head up high / As though he had a huge contempt for Hell' (*Inferno* x 36–7) (fig. 42), or the grandeur of Ulysses' account of his final voyage into the western ocean (*Inferno* xxvi 85–142). We must take care not to be blinded by their glamour. Misguided, and trapped in their own self-regard, these sinners are doomed to repeat for eternity the hollow words and actions which earned

Fig. 42 Gustave Doré (1832–1883), Farinata, Virgil and Dante in the Circle of the Heretics (*Inferno* x). *Dante's Inferno with English text by Cary, illustrated by G. Doré* (London, 1866). Private Collection.

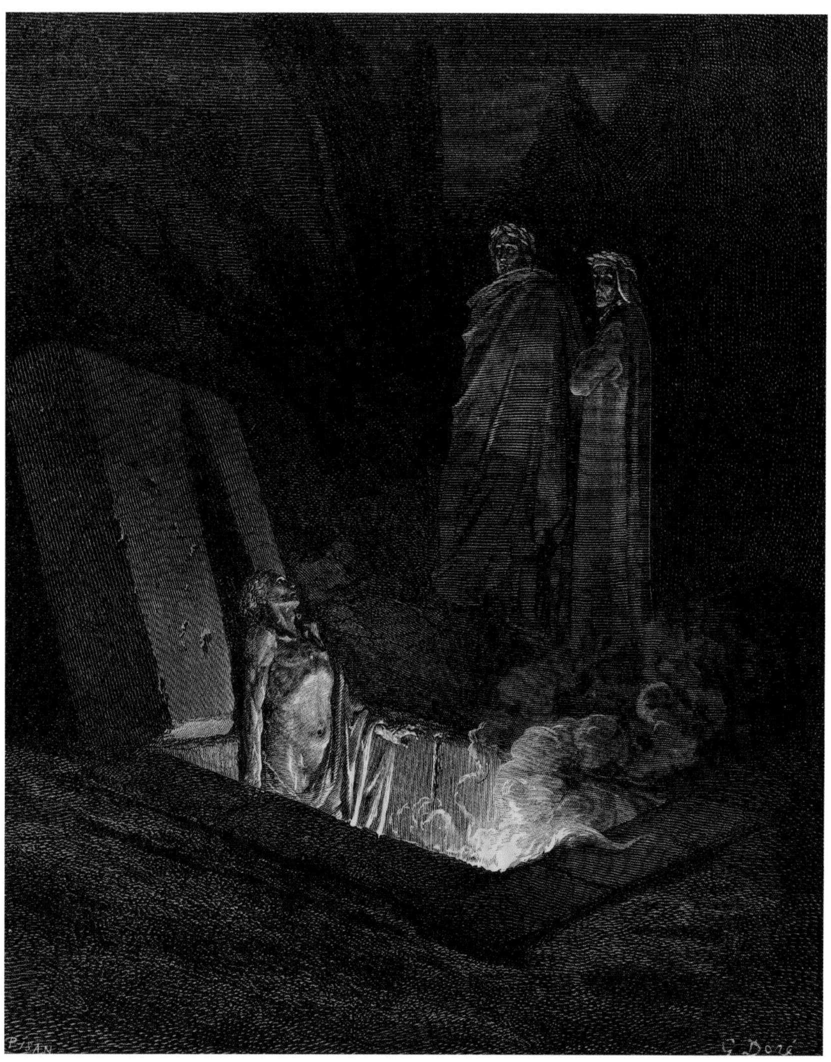

them notoriety in life. Capaneus, who during a siege of Thebes in ancient mythology hurled insults at Jove, speaks for all Hell's residents when he cries: 'What I was when alive, such am I dead!' (*Inferno* xiv 51). The pilgrim, and the reader too, must learn to distinguish between different models of living – between false celebrity and true fame. More than once, the character of Dante, listening to the souls of the renowned men and women encountered in *Inferno*, is moved by sympathy and even tempted to identify, in word and gesture, with their fate. Such insidious power does celebrity work upon us.

Tossed in the winds of Hell's second circle, among those who allowed themselves to be carried away by lust, we encounter the gracious and attractive figure of Francesca of Rimini. We owe her story and she her celebrity entirely to Dante. Married young to an ugly and abusive husband, she fell in

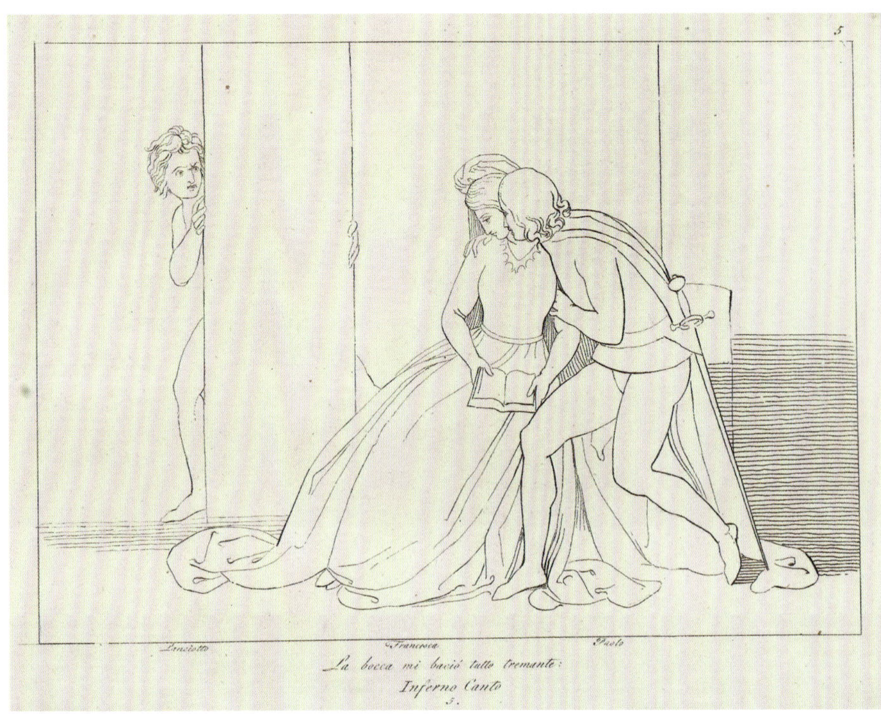

Fig. 43 John Flaxman (1755–1826), Paolo and Francesca (*Inferno* v). *La Divina comedia di Dante Alighieri … composto da Giovanni Flaxman* (Amsterdam, 1793). Bodleian Libraries, University of Oxford, Vet.B5 d.61.

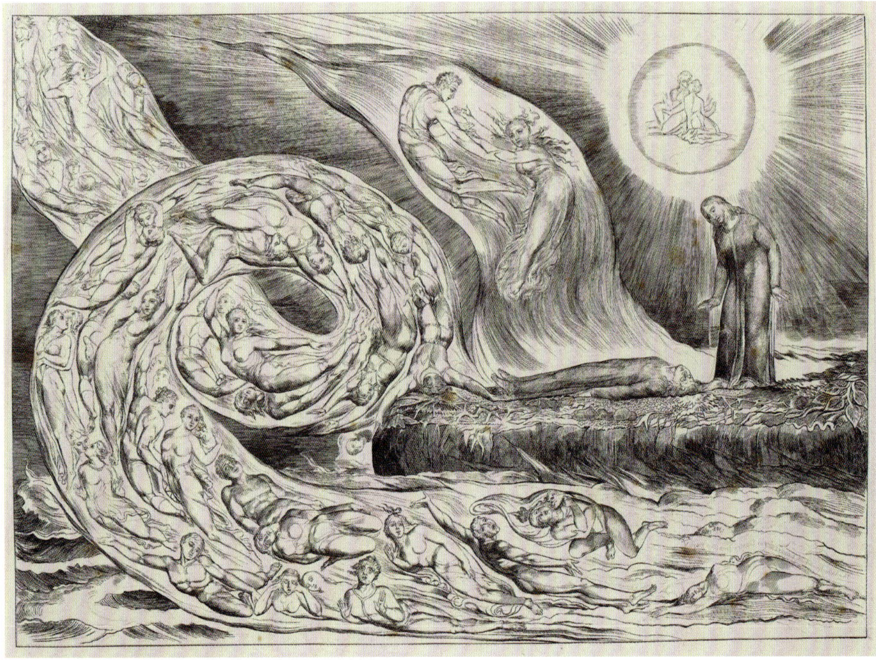

Fig. 44 William Blake (1757–1827), *The Circle of the Lustful: Francesca da Rimini ('The Whirlwind of Lovers'), from Illustrations to Dante's 'Divine Comedy'*, 1827. Engraving and etching, 27.1 × 34.9 cm. Ashmolean Museum (WA1941.27.1). © Ashmolean Museum, University of Oxford.

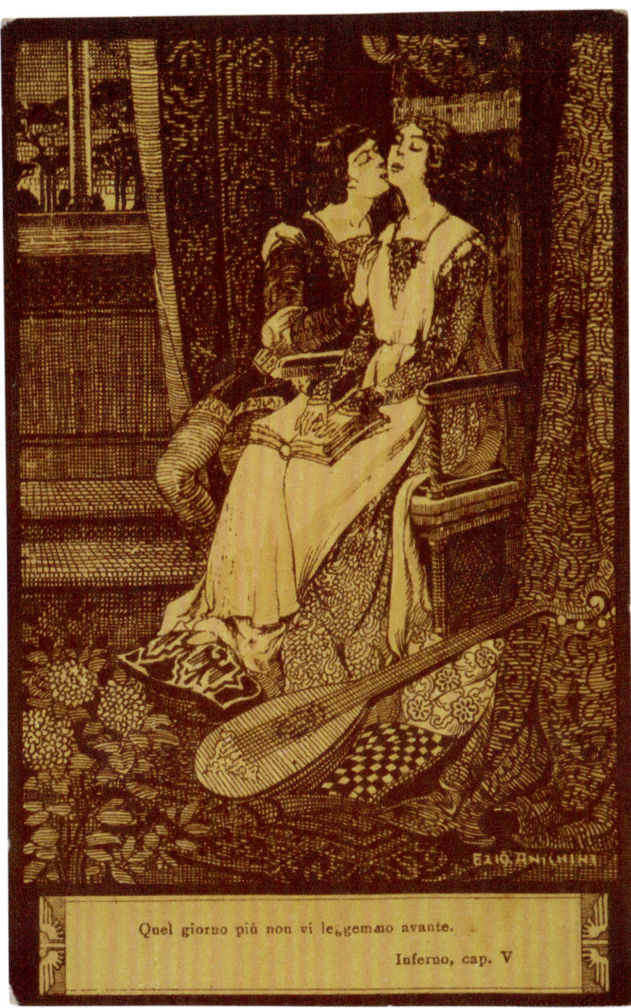

Fig. 45 Ezio Anichini (1886–1948), *Paolo and Francesca*. Postcard, *c.*1910. Private Collection.

love with her handsome brother-in-law, Paolo; the husband killed them both. To the contemporary chronicler of Rimini, this was an exclusively masculine story of dynastic vengeance: 'Paolo was killed by his brother Gianciotto on account of lust.' It is Dante who names Francesca, while in his account Paolo remains unnamed and silent. She alone speaks, and narrates her story as one who (like many other women) had been used as a tool in a dynastic marriage, but who found agency in reading and in the love of another. The poet casts his namesake within the poem in the role of his own younger self, his head full of the literature of romance, offering love-songs at the altar of Venus. The pilgrim senses an affinity from afar, and it is his call which summons Francesca and Paolo who glide, like a pair of doves, to meet him. 'Since you show such sympathy', she says, 'anything you wish to talk about, / Whatever it is, we'll talk of it with you'. In turn, her moving account of the tragic affair prompts Dante, identifying ever more closely with her, to echo the register of her voice, as he asks her to recall how, 'in the time of gentle sighs', the two fell in love. After she describes the – now universally famous – moment in which, while reading together the story of Guinevere's adulterous love for Lancelot, they kissed, Dante faints 'as a body does when dead' (*Inferno* v 79–142) (figs 43–45, and see figs 3–4).

Dante's Francesca is not the wicked woman of contemporary moralists and sermons: she is a person who, with dignity, makes choices, such as any of us might make. Here and throughout the *Comedy*, Dante avoided stereotypes. He did not see evil as an external, satanic force, nor as characteristic of any particular group of people, but as something we do to ourselves when we create false ideals. This is why his visionary account of Hell, Purgatory and Paradise sends us back at every point to the part which image, notoriety, celebrity and fame play in shaping our lives on earth.

IMAGE: WORK IN PROGRESS

About the historical person, Dante Alighieri, we know very little indeed, other than what he chooses to tell us in his writings. Attempts to write his biography might in fact be said to be well-intentioned distractions from the more pertinent project, which is to see how Dante, at each stage of his life, used words to reconstruct his own image. It comes as a shock to realise how far our knowledge is dependent upon his construction. The same is true, as we have seen, of the characters who are conjured up in his poetry. Dante's artifice was in the service of a passionate moral project. His question is always, 'What example should we take for our model of living in the world?' 'What follows', he asks, 'if we pin up the image of this heroic figure, or of that glamorous model?' Dante recognised that we are all implicated in this process of emulation; that we strive to present to our fellow human beings an image of ourselves which corresponds to a type already admired by others. Exemplifying this truth in his own career, Dante more than once re-wrote himself in a new image. At the heart of each self-reconstruction, as the thread which gives continuity to the life, is an evolving idea of love. The embodiment of that notion, as by stages it matures from the youthful sonnets to the *Paradiso*, is Beatrice.

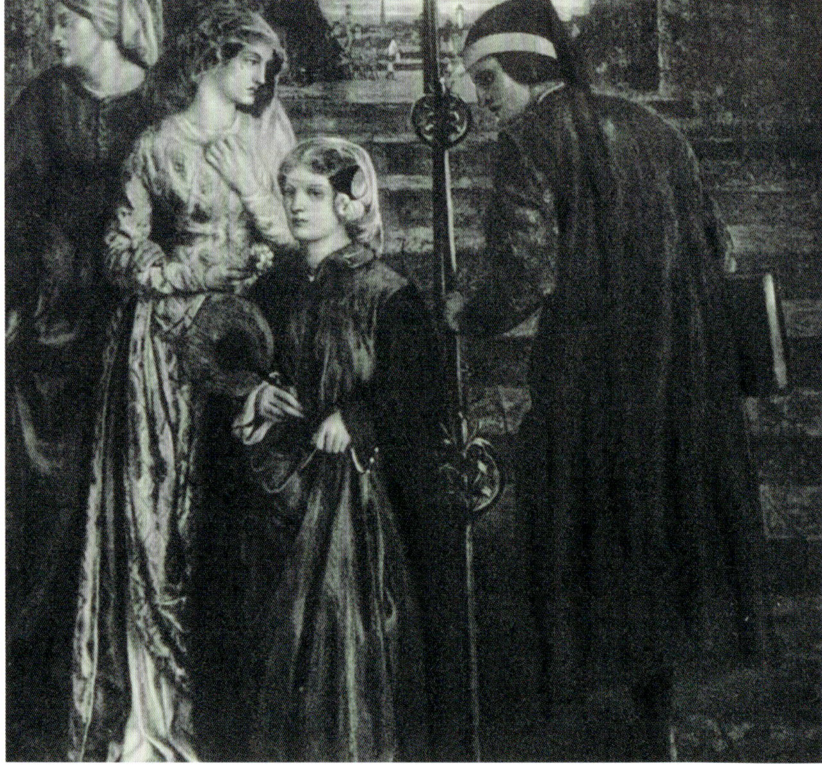

Fig. 46 Dante Gabriel Rossetti (1828–1882), *The Salutation of Beatrice*. Photogravure, *c.*1870–80. Aidan Meller collection, reproduced by permission. Photo: © 2021 Lucy Seal.

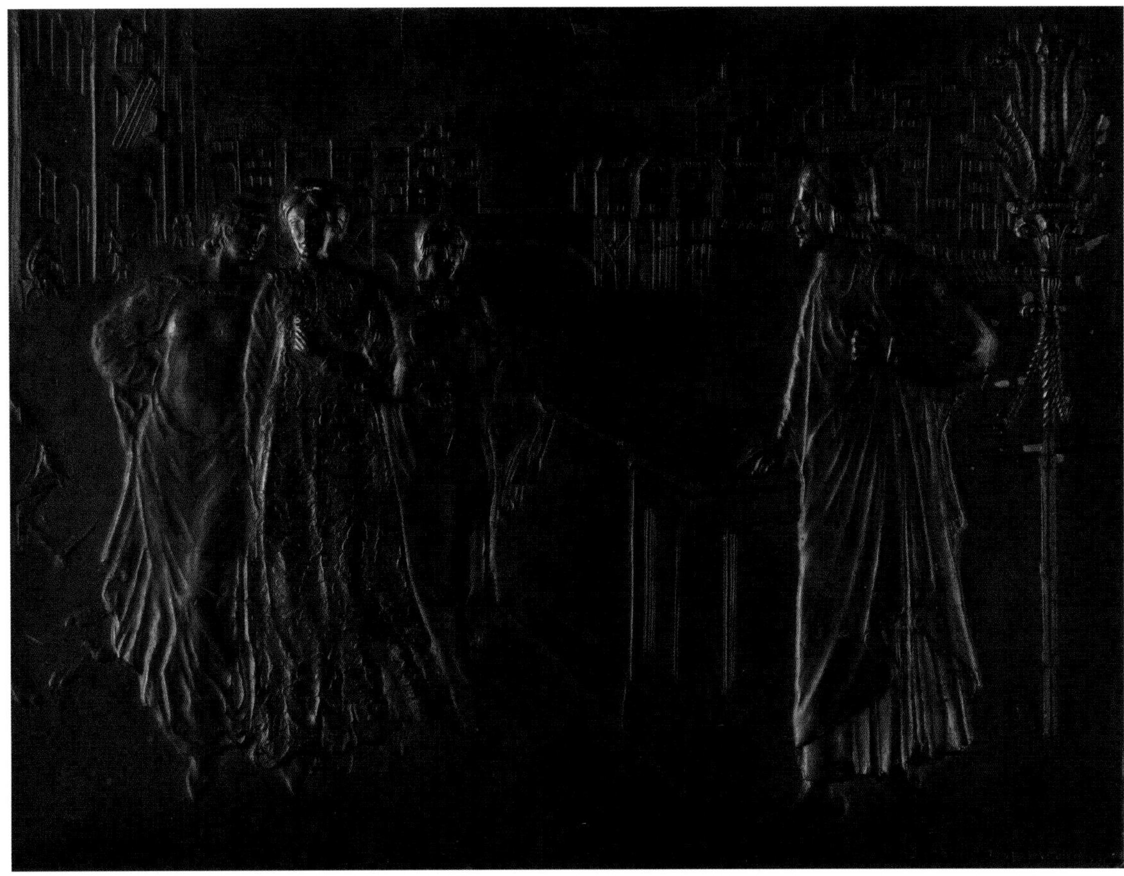

Fig. 47 Giuseppe Gambogi (1862–1938), The Meeting of Dante and Beatrice (after a painting by Henry Holiday). Bronze, 20.0 × 15.5 cm, cast by P. Convalle, Florence, *c.*1890. Private Collection.

Dante's latter-day readers have been drawn, according to changing taste and mood, to different phases of the poet's self-constructed image. The nineteenth century felt a strong affinity for the young love-poet whose tragically curtailed passion for Beatrice was described in his *Vita Nuova*. Scenes from that romance were distilled in images which, widely reproduced, found their way into the homes and the imaginations of thousands. Rossetti's painting (made for William Morris) of *The Salutation of Beatrice*, reproduced as a framed photogravure, hung in countless parlours (fig. 46). A later incident recorded by Dante, in which Beatrice, walking with friends near the Ponte Santa Trìnita, snubbed the poet because of a rumour of his faithlessness, was recreated by Henry Holiday in a painting which became even more famous, and circulated in multiple media (figs 47–49).

Even as he composed his *Vita Nuova* (to which he also gave the Latin title *Vita nova*), in his late twenties, Dante was revising the profile of his image as a poet. Taking a selection of his earlier poetry, which had previously circulated amongst his fellow rhymesters of love, the book presented an elevated commentary which could lend philosophical underpinning and ethical weight to the work and to its author. The climax of the narrative

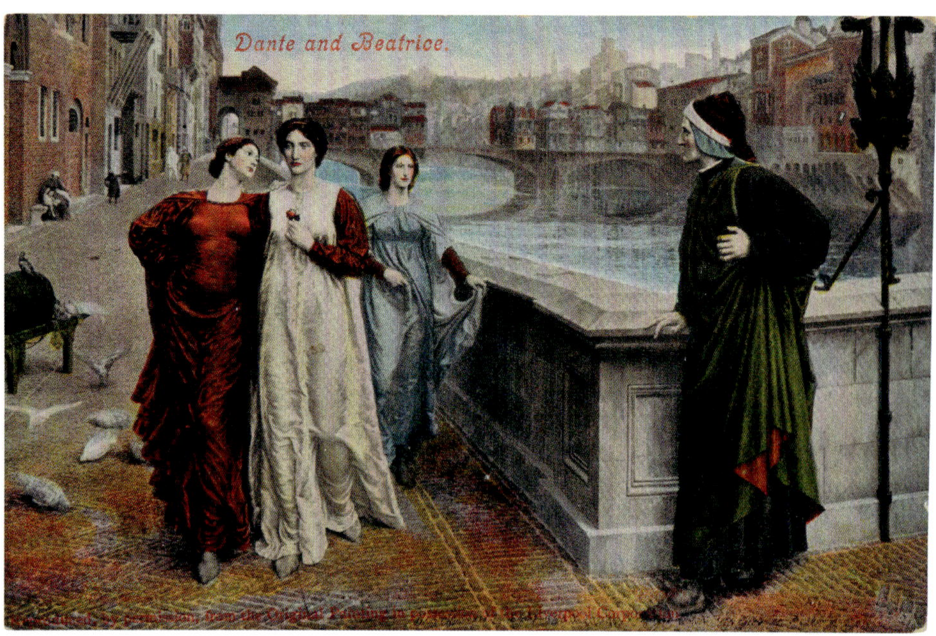

Fig. 48 *Meeting of Dante and Beatrice* (after Henry Holiday). Postcard, early 20th century. Private Collection.

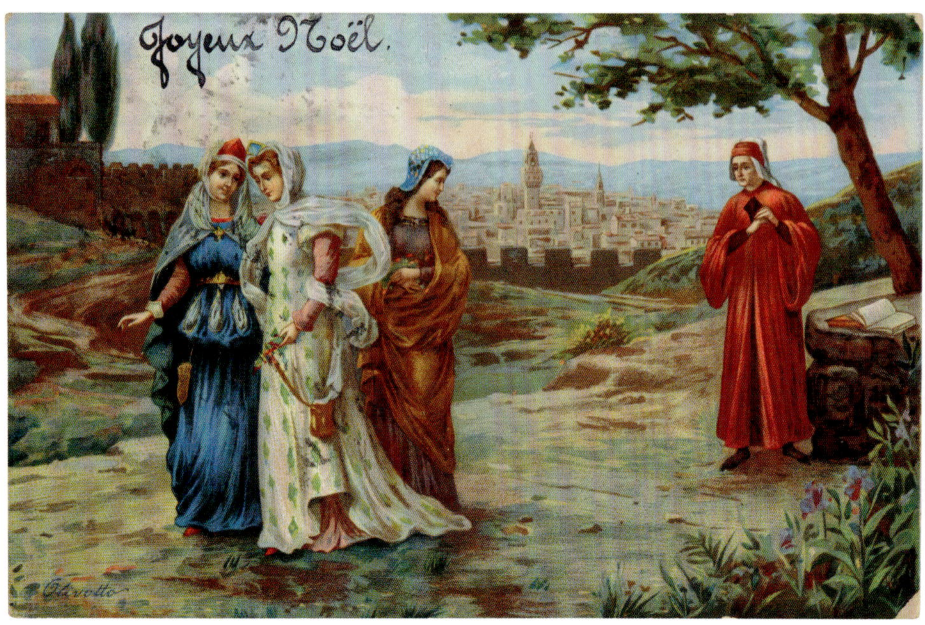

Fig. 49 *Meeting of Dante and Beatrice*. Postcard with Christmas greeting, early 20th century. Private Collection.

is the death of Beatrice, which leaves Dante reflecting on further ways in which he might transfigure the relationship. He records that on the first anniversary of her death, he was commemorating her by painting an angel, when visitors interrupted him: a scene evoked by Dante Gabriel Rossetti (to whom the subject had been recommended by John Ruskin). Dante wrote that on this occasion 'another was with me', which prompted the Pre-Raphaelite painter to include himself as the poet's friend (fig. 50). Dante's ultimate response to the loss of Beatrice was to be the *Comedy*.

The *Comedy*, which Dante composed during his exile from Florence between about 1306 and his death in 1321, is above all an account of how the pilgrim learns to see clearly, and so becomes able to distinguish between appearance and reality. Lost in the dark wood, he is rescued initially by Virgil, who points out that Dante is unable to see things as they truly are (*Inferno* II 48). Virgil's intervention was prompted by the prayers of Beatrice, and it is to Beatrice herself that Virgil delivers Dante on their arrival, at the summit of the mountain of Purgatory, in the Earthly Paradise. This meeting in Dante's vision, after a number of years since Beatrice's death, is momentous. She reassures him that his eyes, now, are not deceiving him: 'Guardaci ben! ben son, ben son Beatrice' ('Look at me well! For I am

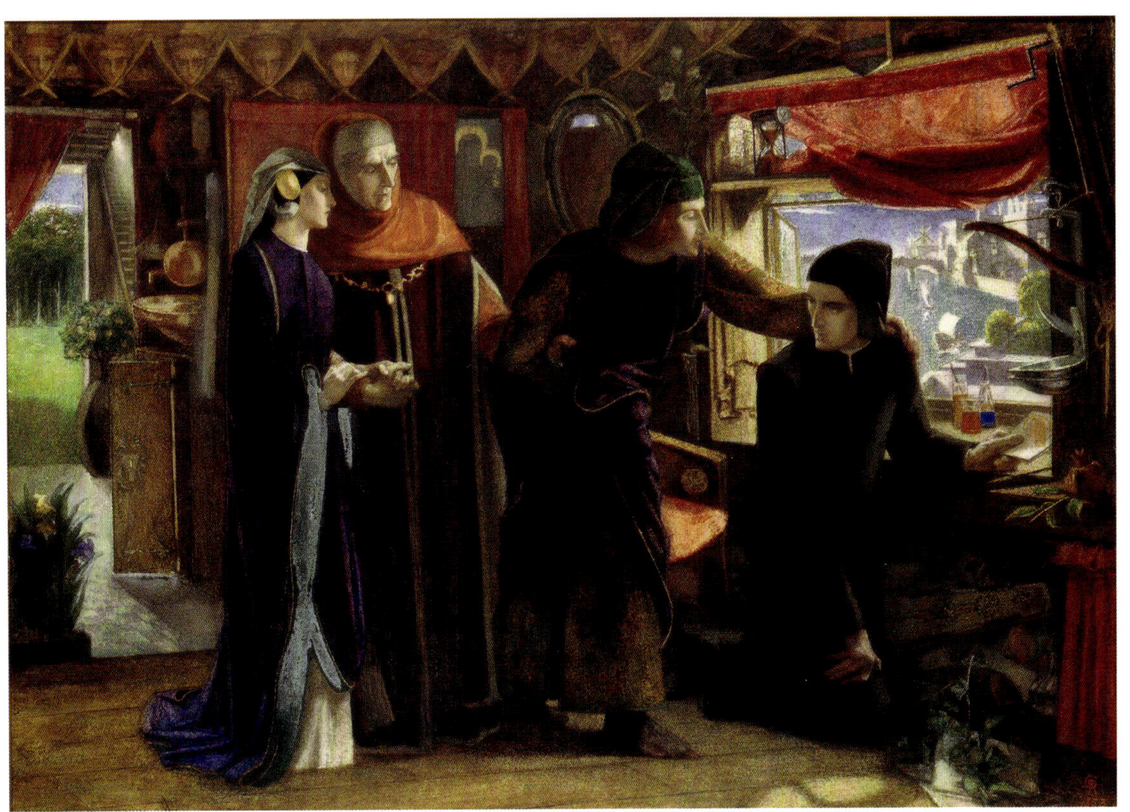

Fig. 50 Dante Gabriel Rossetti (1828–1882), *Dante drawing an Angel on the Anniversary of Beatrice's Death*, 1853. Watercolour and bodycolour on paper, 42 × 61 cm. Ashmolean Museum (WA1894.16). © Ashmolean Museum, University of Oxford.

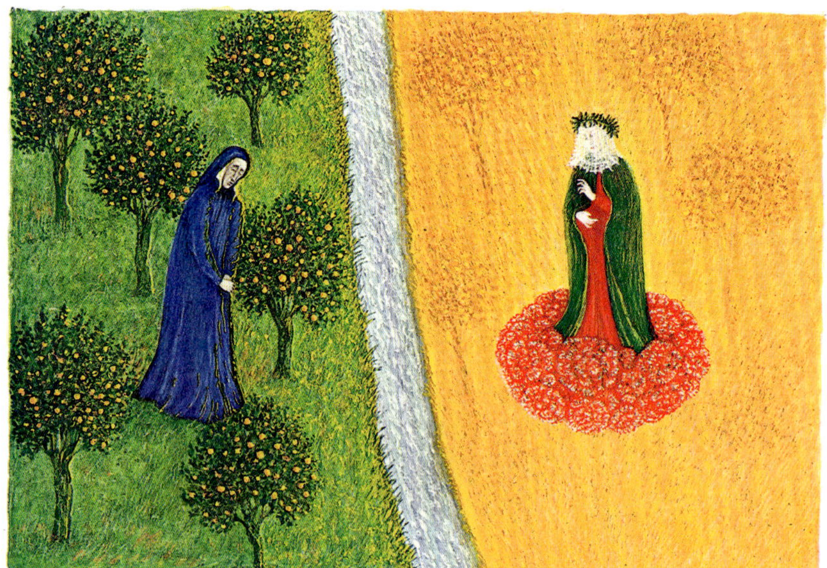

Fig. 51 Monika Beisner (b. 1942), 'Look at me well! For I am Beatrice' (*Purgatorio* XXX 73). With the artist's permission.

Beatrice') (*Purgatorio* XXX 73) (fig. 51). To his embarrassment, she sternly reproves him for pursuing relationships following her death, motivated by selfish lust rather than a spiritually generous love. The Beatrice Dante now gazes at is a guide for living above any yet encountered. 'Regal of bearing, rigorous, steadfast', she looks down at Dante from her chariot, which she paces 'like an admiral' on the deck of his ship: the figure of Beatrice, a paragon rising above all earthly figures of fame, transcends conventional categories of gender. And now begins the final phase of the purification of Dante's sight, which is brought about through the eyes of Beatrice.

When they first arrive together in Paradise, only Beatrice is able to look directly at the heavens – to 'gaze unflinchingly into the sun / As never any eagle could' (*Paradiso* I 47–8). Gradually, however, she teaches Dante to look with her at the heavenly lights. When, with an explosion of radiance, Christ appears, and Dante again is overwhelmed, Beatrice urges him to look first at her – 'Open your eyes – see me more beautiful' – and then at 'the splendour of Christ's rays' (*Paradiso* XXIII 46, 72). Dante finds that it is only through his relationship with another, sincerely loved and therefore clearly perceived, that it becomes possible to glimpse, like the rays of the sun breaking through a cloud, the divine light which penetrates and illuminates the universe. Redemption can only be a collaborative and generous relationship of love (figs 51–55).

The spiritual blindness of the damned in Hell (described by Virgil as 'a world where all is blind' (*Inferno* IV 13)) derives from their preoccupation with themselves that has led them to project the narrow and false ideals

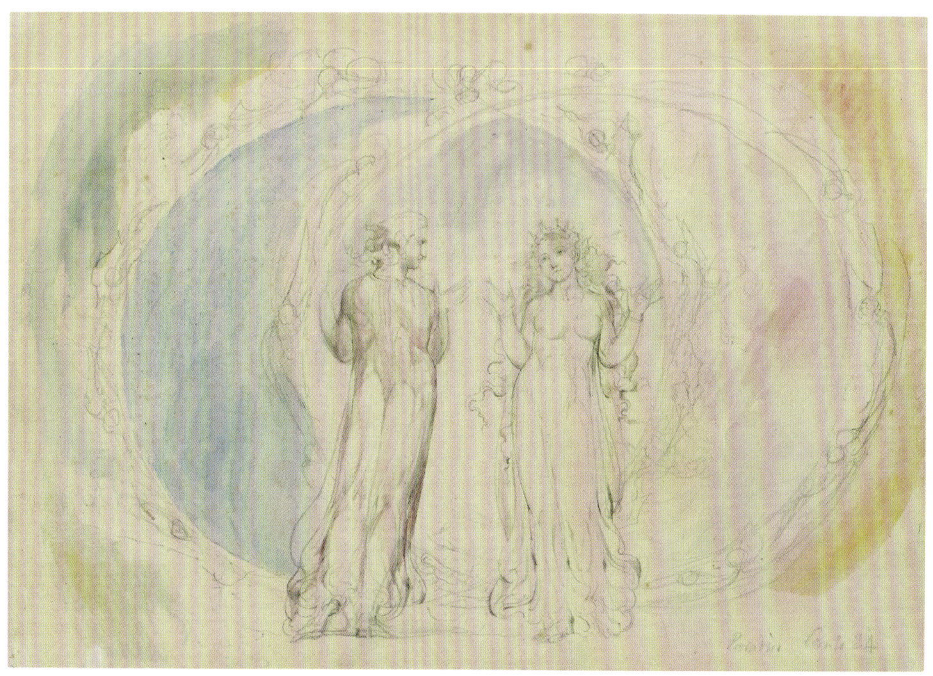

Fig. 52 William Blake (1757–1827), *Beatrice and Dante in Gemini, amid the Spheres of Flame (illustration to the 'Divine Comedy', Paradiso XXIV)*, 1825–27. Watercolour and some pen and black ink over graphite and black chalk, 35.5 × 51 cm. Ashmolean Museum (WA1918.5). © Ashmolean Museum, University of Oxford.

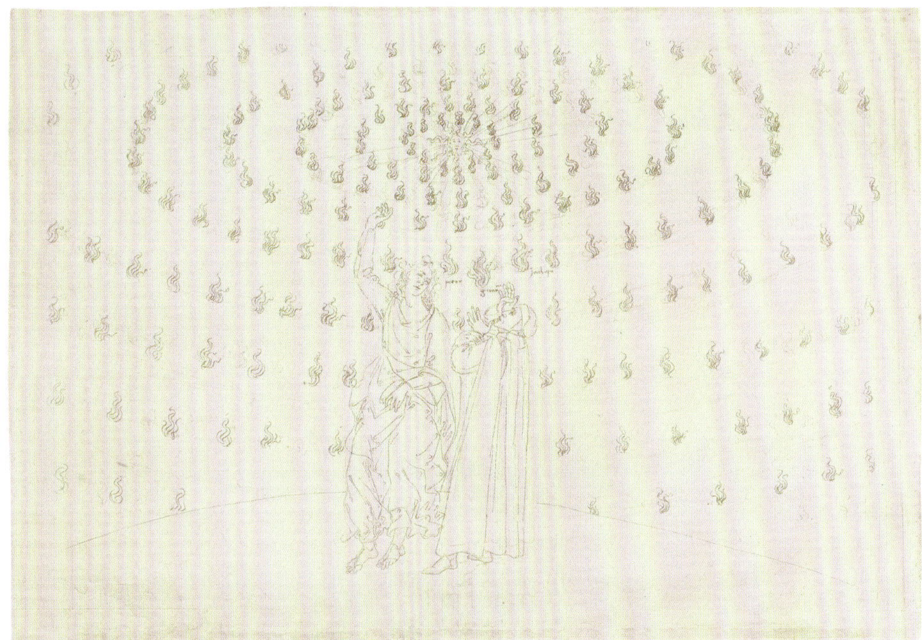

Fig. 53 Sandro Botticelli (1445–1510), illustration to Paradiso XXVI (1480s), facsimile. *Zeichnungen von Sandro Botticelli zu Dantes Goettlicher Komoedie: nach den Originalen im K. Kupferstichkabinett zu Berlin* (Berlin: G. Grote'sche Verlagsbuchhandlung, 1887). Taylor Institution Library: REP.X.55 (plates).

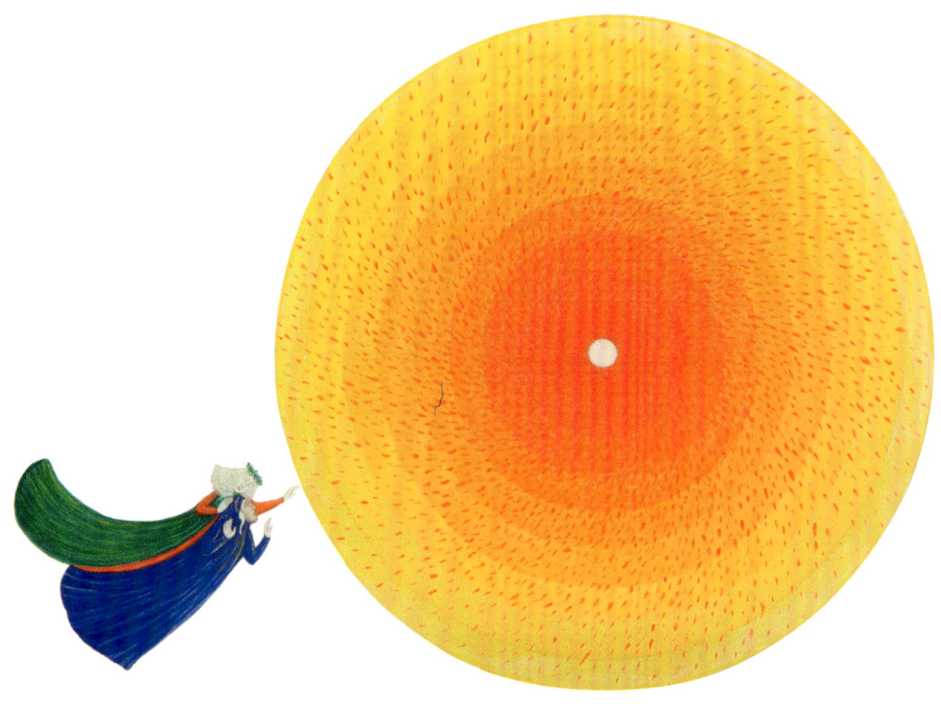

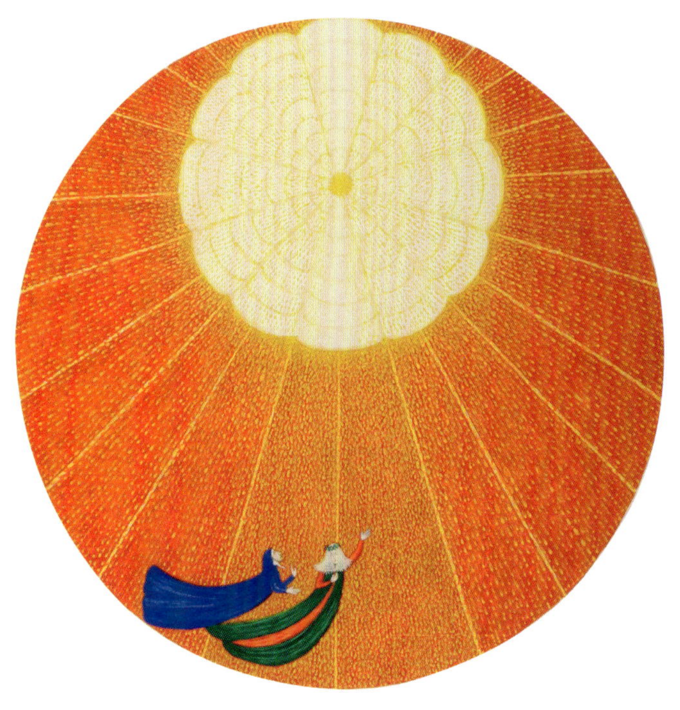

Opposite top:
Fig. 54 Monika Beisner (b. 1942), The Nine Orders of Angels (*Paradiso* XXVIII). With the artist's permission.

Opposite bottom:
Fig. 55 Monika Beisner (b. 1942), The Mystic Rose (*Paradiso* XXXI). With the artist's permission.

upon which they have modelled their own lives. The whole of Dante's journey through the *Comedy* is a process of learning to perceive the fatal limitations of those models, and instead to put trust in the virtuous souls whom he meets. These include all of the characters encountered in the upper realms of the vision, whether they are patiently working through their penance in Purgatory or radiant in enjoyment of their particular place in Paradise. In each, the pilgrim finds something new to admire and to emulate; and they in turn take pleasure in helping both him and one another. In Dante's vision, redemption from the hell of self-love can only be attained through openness to the love of others, which is epitomised in the gaze he exchanges with Beatrice. The ultimate ideal, in this perspective, is communal. The individual in isolation may acquire a certain worldly celebrity. But only the community which is bound by mutual love can hope for true and lasting fame.

Notes

1 John Ruskin, *The Stones of Venice*, 3 vols (London, 1853), vol. iii, p. 158.
2 Jorge Luis Borges, in *Borges at Eighty. Conversations*, ed. W. Barnstone (Bloomington, Indiana, 1982), p. 93.
3 Ovid, *Metamorphoses*, tr. A.D. Melville (Oxford, 1986), xv, lines 877–9 (p. 379).
4 Giovanni Boccaccio, *Life of Dante* [*c*.1370], in *The Early Lives of Dante*, tr. P.H. Wicksteed (London, 1904), p. 53.
5 Charles Chaplin, *My Autobiography* (London, 1964), pp. 287–8.
6 Giorgio Vasari, *Life of Pierino da Vinci*, in his *Lives of the Painters, Sculptors and Architects*, tr. G. du C. de Vere and ed. D. Ekserdjian, 2 vols (London, 1996), vol. ii, p. 261.

FURTHER READING

Dante Alighieri, *The Divine Comedy*, tr. J.G. Nichols (London: Alma Classics, 2012). Quotations in the text are taken from this translation, with the kind permission of the publishers.

Dante, *La Divina Commedia*, ed. N. Sapegno, 3 vols. (Florence: La Nuova Italia, 1985)

Dante, *Vita nova*, tr. A. Frisardi (Northwestern UP, 2012)

Peter Hainsworth and David Robey, *Dante. A Very Short Introduction* (Oxford: Oxford UP, 2015)

Peter Hawkins, *Dante: A Brief History* (Oxford: Blackwell, 2006)

Nick Havely, *Dante* (Oxford: Blackwell, 2007)

Guy P. Raffa, *Dante's Bones. How a Poet Invented Italy* (Cambridge, Mass.: Harvard UP, 2020)

Robin Kirkpatrick, *Dante: The Divine Comedy* (Cambridge: Cambridge UP, 1987)

Rachel Jacoff, ed., *The Cambridge Companion to Dante* (Cambridge: Cambridge UP, 1993)

Zygmunt G. Barański and Simon Gilson, eds., *The Cambridge Companion to Dante's 'Commedia'* (Cambridge: Cambridge UP, 2019)

ACKNOWLEDGEMENTS

This modest contribution to the extensive literature on Dante is indebted to the keenly attentive and resourceful editorship of Dec McCarthy. Stephen Hebron's design skills are beyond price, and I cannot sufficiently thank him for his elegance and taste. It has been a pleasure to collaborate with Catherine Whistler, Matthew Winterbottom, Caroline Palmer, Katherine Wodehouse and Catriona Pearson at the Ashmolean Museum, and with Sallyanne Gilchrist and Martin Kauffmann at the Bodleian Libraries. Profound thanks are also due to Aidan Meller for his financial support of this publication. For kind permission to quote from the translation of Dante's *Comedy* by J.G. Nichols, I am grateful to the publishers of Alma Classics. For visual discoveries and infinite conversation, I thank Jane Garnett, 'my sweet and loving guide'.